# children helping children:
## Teaching Students to Become Friendly Helpers

by
Robert D. Myrick
and
Robert P. Bowman

Copyright © 1981
EDUCATIONAL MEDIA CORPORATION®
P.O. Box 21311
Minneapolis, Minnesota 55421

Library of Congress Catalog Card No. 81-82900

ISBN 0-932796-09-5

Printing (Last Digit)

9 8 7 6 5 4

No part of this book may be reproduced or used in any form without the expressed permission of the publisher in writing. Manufactured in the United States of America.

*Production editor —*

**Don L. Sorenson**

*Graphic design—*

**Earl Sorenson**

*Illustrations—*

**Mary M. McKee**

**Dedication**

**Carl and Ferris Fisher**

grandparents and significant facilitators of a young boy

**Clint Edward Geer**

grandson and a young boy becoming a future facilitator

# Table of Contents

**Chapter I Growing up in a Changing World**   1

   Student Facilitators   3
   The Challenges of a Changing World   4
      *The Land of the Berry-Hoppers*   9
      Table 1.1   14

**Chapter II Children as Helpers**   15

   Early Roots in Education   16
   Students in Helping Roles   20
   Peer Facilitator Programs   33
   Students as Helpers: Some Benefits   44

**Chapter III Begining a Student Facilitator Program**   47

   Step 1: Making a Committment   49
      The Need for the Program   50
      The Purpose of the Program   51
      The Program's Objectives   53
         Table 3.1   54
         Table 3.2   56
      Important Concepts and Skills   57
      The Helping Relationships   58
      Some New Helpers   59
         Table 3.3   61
      Program Trainer or Coordinator   77

**Chapter IV Getting Organized**   79

   Step 2: Forming a Plan   80
   Step 3: Enlisting Support   90
   Step 4: Selecting Student Facilitators   96
      Figure 4.1 An Invitation   97
      Figure 4.2 An Acceptance Letter   100
      Figure 4.3 An Alternate's Letter   101
      Figure 4.4 A Student Facilitator's Contract   104

**Chapter V Training Student Facilitators**   105

   Step 5: Training the Facilitators   105
      The Training Sessions   108
      Organization of the Training Sessions   111
         Table 5.1 Summary of Training Sessions   112

| | |
|---|---|
| Sessions One and Two | 116 |
| *Friendly Helpers and Helping Characteristics* | |
| Sessions Three and Four | 121 |
| *The Careful Listener* | |
| Sessions Five, Six, Seven and Eight | 127 |
| *Making Helpful Responses* | |
| Session Nine | 135 |
| *Looking at the Helping Process* | |
| Session Ten | 139 |
| *Preparing for Beginning Projects* | |
| Sessions Eleven, Twelve and Thirteen | 142 |
| *Helping Solve Problems* | |
| Sessions Fourteen and Fifteen | 148 |
| *Giving Feedback* | |
| Sessions Sixteen and Seventeen | 154 |
| *Looking at Yourself and Others* | |
| Session Eighteen | 159 |
| *Putting it all Together* | |
| Sessions Nineteen and Twenty | 161 |
| *Becoming a Friendly Helper* | |
| Supplemental and Additional Sessions | 166 |

## Chapter VI Implementing and Supervising Projects — 167

| | |
|---|---|
| Step 6: Implementing and Supervising Projects | 167 |
| Implementing Helping Projects | 168 |
| Student Assistant Projects | 177 |
| Tutor Projects | 183 |
| Special Friend Projects | 189 |
| Small Group Leader Projects | 194 |
| "My Friends and Me" | 204 |
| Facilitators as Co-leaders | 210 |
| Supervision | 211 |

## Chapter VII Assessing and Evaluating Progress — 217

| | |
|---|---|
| Step 7: Assessing and Evaluating Progress | 217 |
| Why Assess and Evaluate? | 218 |
| Sources of Information and Evaluation | 219 |
| Four Areas of Assessment | 222 |
| Figure 7.1 Attitudes Toward Others Survey | 223 |
| Figure 7.2 Assertiveness Assessment Scale | 225 |

| | |
|---|---|
| Figure 7.3 Student Behavior Inventory | 227 |
| Figure 7.4 Facilitator Skills and Concepts Test | 229 |
| Figure 7.5 Facilitator Skills and Concepts Test | 231 |
| Figure 7.6 Facilitator Skills Tally Card | 234 |
| Figure 7.7 Side One, Tape 3—Grace and Melissa | 235 |
| Figure 7.8 Facilitator Effectiveness Test | 238 |

## Chapter VIII Trainers as Facilitators and Learners — 241

| | |
|---|---|
| Figure 8.1 Trainer Rating Scale | 242 |
| Being a Successful Trainer | 246 |
| *The Case of James* | 248 |
| What Trainers Have Said | 252 |
| What Others Have Said | 253 |
| And Now... | 254 |

## Appendix — 255

| | |
|---|---|
| Supplemental Activities Chapter I | |
| Learning About Resistance | 255 |
| Feeling Word Search (II) | 256 |
| Supplemental Activities Chapter II | |
| The Gossip Game | 258 |
| Ten Questions | 259 |
| Supplemental Activities Chapter III | |
| Pass the Pencil | 260 |
| H.O.T. Triads | 262 |
| Supplemental Activities Chapter IV | |
| Dear Abby | 262 |
| Alternatives and Consequences | 263 |
| Supplemental Activites Chapter V | |
| Feedback Go Around | 265 |
| Positive Superlatives | 266 |
| Supplemental Activities Chapter VI | |
| Circles, Squares or Triangles? | 267 |
| The Ideal Student | 268 |
| Supplemental Activities Chapter VII | |
| Unfinished Sentences | 269 |
| The Helping Roles | 270 |

## List of Recommended Resources — 271

## Bibliography — 273

# Preface

This book is written for elementary and middle school counselors, teachers and principals who want to improve the learning climate in their schools. Along with its companion book, *Becoming a Friendly Helper,* it is designed to help young students take a more active role in the learning and helping process. Together, they offer an organized program in which children become more effective helpers with each other.

Student facilitator programs have received increased attention within the past several years, especially at the secondary level. They are an outgrowth of the developmental guidance movement, first described by early contributors to elementary school counseling such as Verne Faust and Don Dinkmeyer.

They are a logical response to the high counselor and teacher student ratios in most schools. In addition, they provide a learning experience in which the best theories and methodologies in education are integrated.

This book and its companion are the first of their kind for elementary school students and can be easily adapted for those in middle schools. The books help young people to communicate more effectively, solve problems and make decisions more efficiently, and assume more responsibility for their actions. In a sense, it is a leadership program in which students help build a positive learning atmosphere for themselves and others.

There are many people who have assisted us in our efforts. It is impossible to recognize everyone to whom we are indebted. However, a few have been especially helpful.

Among the several professional educators and writers who helped stimulate our thinking were: Dr. Tom Erney, Dr. Jim Gumaer, Dr. Al Milliren, as well as others cited in Chapter II of this book.

There were several counselors, principals, teachers and students who reacted to our ideas, experimented with training activities and projects, and offered encouragement, including: elementary and middle school counselors, Beth Dovell, Liz Parker, Jack Carter, Karen Price, Susan Ream, Bob Poston, Shari Campbell, Kathy LeBlanc, Marta Konik, Rosemary Collins, Dot Thomas, Bonnie Baker, and Jacque Cake (Gainesville, Flordia); administrator, Lawrence Head; teachers, Lori Kosaka, Charlene Meyers, Kim Griffith; and student facilitators such as Ulisses Gutierrez, Claudia Ramirez and Grace McKinnon (Bellwood, Illinois).

In addition, there were many counselors and teachers who listened to our presentations at state and national conferences, talked with us about our ideas, and described some of their own interests and projects. Just as important were occasions when people took time after our programs and workshops to express their interest, concern and enthusiasm.

Appreciation is also expressed to Dr. Linda Myrick, who as guidance coordinator for Alachua County Schools, Gainesville, Florida, made it possible to bring counselors together so that we might study and experiment with different ideas and activities. She also reacted to parts of the manuscript, offered timely support, and insisted that the book be finished before becoming an enclycopedia of developmental guidance.

Likewise, Denise Jud Bowman was supportive, offered encouragement, and shared in the excitement of the project. Her patience and her understanding of the writers were severely tested, but she became a sustaining force so that their work could be completed.

Finally, we wish to thank Dr. Don Sorenson, who believed in the value of the books from the beginning and who, with Earl Sorenson, provided the technical assistance to bring our program and ideas to you.

**RDM**
**RPB**

# Chapter I
# Growing Up in a Changing World

Ken was a third year counselor in Spring Forest Elementary School. During his first year, he started a developmental guidance program with an emphasis upon group counseling and working with teachers in their classrooms. He liked his work and the favorable support he received from his principal and teachers. Professional colleagues envied his position and Ken looked forward to doing even more things.

About mid-year, however, Ken began to experience some frustration. Perhaps it had always been there, creeping slowly into his work, but he sensed something was missing. There were many things that he wanted to do, so many students who needed special attention and so little time to accomplish his goals.

One day Ken talked with Angela, a sixth grade student who met with him because of some personal problems that were affecting her attitude at school. He liked Angela and enjoyed working with her. She was doing better and his work with her was almost finished. Yet, Angela could still benefit from some additional counseling experiences. It was a dilemma for Ken.

He considered putting her into a group, but concluded that Angela was so easy to talk with and skilled in her own way that she might not get much from a beginning counseling group. Then, he started thinking about how Angela might co-lead a group with him. The experience would give her some recognition, some responsibility and an opportunity to practice some listening skills that she learned from individual counseling. Ken decided to let her co-lead the group with him. Angela was delighted to be his helper.

A few weeks later, Ken noted the group's progress. He concluded that Angela's presence contributed to the group's success. Her comments were often timely and she provided a link for him—an adult—to the young group members. On several occasions students turned to Angela, looking for her reactions, listening to her comments and feeling the impact of her participation. Angela was also an attentive listener and showed a keen interest in the group. Ken mused, "I'll bet Angela could have led the group by herself... well, maybe with a little bit of my help. But, she was great!"

Later, this same thought reoccurred. Ken thought about it some more and decided that Angela could, with some instruction and practice, lead a small group of younger students through some structured activities. She could be his helper, a kind of a counselor assistant. As a peer, she might even be able to facilitate the group more than an adult.

This experience led to other students being considered for a peer program that was slowly beginning to take form, a program where students worked as facilitators or special helpers to other students. Ken and his students had unknowingly become a part of an important and promising new movement in education— student facilitator programs.

## Student Facilitators

What is a student facilitator? *A student facilitator is a young person in school who uses helping concepts and skills to assist other students—and sometimes adults—to think about ideas and feelings, to explore alternatives to situations, and to make responsible decisions.* The term is used synonomously with other titles such as peer facilitator and peer counselor.

Student facilitators, however, are not advice-givers or problem-solvers for someone else. They are not certified counselors or psychologists. Rather, *they are sensitive listeners who are able to give appropriate feedback and encouragement to others.*

There are student facilitators at all grade levels. Sometimes they work in cross-age projects and in such roles as teacher/counselor assistant, tutor, friendly helper, and small group leader. Regardless of roles their objectives are usually the same: *to promote personal and academic growth through positive relationships.*

Many different types of student facilitator programs exist in the nation's schools. Some have developed with little planning, but they are still relatively successful because of the caring, commitment and energy of the people involved. Yet, many times, too much is left to chance and hope. Some programs have evolved from special projects or circumstances in particular schools. Again, there is too often a lack of organization or focus. These programs are frequently more limited in scope.

Finally, there are a few programs, most of which are just beginning, that have clear objectives and have an organized set of training sessions and projects for students. Moreover, these programs have a coordinator, trainer, or director who assumes responsibility for organization, training, supervision, helping projects and evaluation. It is this latter approach that is most successful.

Until recently, most organized student facilitator programs were found in colleges or secondary schools. With the help of counselors and teachers, more programs have begun to appear in elementary and middle schools.

## The Challenges of a Changing World

The pace of living is faster than it was twenty five years ago. The world is more complex. It is as confusing as it is remarkable. In the past quarter-century some dramatic events, inventions, discoveries and social movements revolutionized society. They also provided us with many problems and challenges.

There is little doubt that electronic wizardry, in the form of sophisticated computers and processing systems, will transform nearly every aspect of society in the 1980s. In the next few years, microelectronic intelligence is likely to be incorporated into almost every product large enough to contain it. We will be living in a world of "smart" machines.

These machines will do wonderous things for us and we will have access to information from thousands of sources all over the world. Yet, more information and rapid telecommunication systems will not provide any final answers to human history. To the contrary, the most important questions and answers to the future rest in the communication skills and patterns among people themselves. Despite immense technological achievements, life's decisions are made by people who are affected by their attitudes, values, expectations and relationships with others.

While modern technology continues to produce more technology and marvelous inventions that become household items, there is a growing concern that the signs of the times are foreboding ones. Advanced technology has produced the weaponry that threatens world security. It has also created social changes that are having a pronounced impact upon children and youth of the country, the nation's future.

Some significant social trends are emerging and problem areas are being identified. While there are always limitations to research procedures and available data, the biennial report entitled *The Status of Children and Families* (1979), published by the U.S. Department of Health and Human Services, is a document that demands our attention. It emphasizes the stress and strain of growing up in a changing world.

One of the most important changes for families is that more women are working outside the home than ever before.

- Almost 50% of all children have mothers who work outside the home.
- Approximately seven million children are left behind when mothers go to work outside the home.
- Of women with school-age children, 62% are working outside the home.
- Working mothers with preschool children increased from 14% to 39% between 1950 and 1976. Almost 45% now work outside the home.

Many of these women are not working for the joy of it. Soaring inflation and economic factors frequently force many women to work outside the home. Some have no choice, as they are the primary breadwinners.

The family structure has changed a great deal and fewer children are living with two parent families, mainly because of the increasing number of divorces.

- One out of three marriages now end in divorce.
- Between 20% and 30% of children growing up in the 1970s will eventually have divorced parents.
- Another 5% to 10% will be living with a single parent because of annulment, separation, or death.

Although it is difficult to know the effects of divorce upon children, stress in a parental relationship causes stress on the child. Children of divorce have generally been considered as more likely than others to be low-achievers in school, delinquent, and psychologically disturbed.

Today's population tends to be a mobile one. Even when families stay together as a unit, they are often on the move.

- In 1978, 54% of the children, ages 3-4, and 43%, ages 5-9, moved during the previous three year period.
- About one out of every five families moves each year.

Although about 25% of these families remain within the same county, nevertheless, there is an uprooting. This produces a transitional stress for children that can be detrimental to their personal and academic growth. Children are also running away from home and schools in increasing numbers.

— In 1976 over 733,000 young people ages 1-17 left home annually without parental consent.

— In 1977, the problem reached such proportions and concern as to promote the passage of the *Runaway Youth Act,* which was designed to help youth who were living on the streets and subject to dangerous encounters.

For some children, running away seems like the only solution to the problems that face them in school or in their families. In addition, many children run away as a result of continual abuse or neglect from family members.

— Some estimates indicate that 4-5 million children are abused each year.

— Each year about 2,000 to 5,000 children are killed as a result of child abuse.

— Abuse recurs regularly in approximately 50% of cases where no help is given and in 35% of these cases a child will be injured severely.

— Even though laws requiring mandatory reporting of child abuse were enacted in 1974, many cases go unreported and legal action is often stalled or stymied.

Yet, for all of these abused and neglected children, business is expected to proceed as usual when they enter the classroom. Their plight is often unknown even though it burdens their learning and impairs their relationships with others. For some, the burden is too great.

— More than one out of ten teenagers and young adults who died in 1976 did so by means of suicide.

— Of these, more than 80% made previous attempts and gave warning of their depression.

— The suicide rate among young people has increased 20% since 1950.

One may wonder why these young people did not seek out help from responsible adults and mental health agencies. While it is true that such agencies have increased in number over the years, there are still too few children being seen.

- In 1975 about 655,000 children under the age of 18 were admitted to an organized mental health facility.
- Yet, it represented only 1% of the children in the U. S. when no less than 10% to 30% are estimated to be in need of such help.
- Referral lists from schools to mental health agencies are long and only about 20% are ever seen beyond the initial interview.

Some students use alcohol, drugs and acting out behaviors to deal with their anxiety. The illicit use of drugs among young people has increased. Likewise, the number of crimes committed by young people has risen.

- Since 1957 there has been a gradual increase in the rates of young people being processed in the juvenile courts. In 1976, there were slightly more than two million arrests of persons between ages 11 and 17.
- About 7% of the 28.8 million youth were involved in crimes that took them to court.

In light of the changing family and the increasing number of problems facing young people, more attention has been given to the schools, both public and private, as one place where crises facing young people can be encountered. But, schools are also experiencing difficulties and too many only add more stress and tension to the situation.

- The lack of discipline in the schools continues to be the number one concern of parents who respond to Gallup polls.
- Racial tensions have created additional stresses among students and parents. For example, buses have been used to desegregate and intergrate school systems. However, in many schools, the racial stress continues or is increased.

- Violence and vandalism has sometimes been an outgrowth of tensions at schools which emerge from name calling, racial and religious prejudice, stereotyping, and personal slurs.

Guidance services are limited in the schools. Teachers have large classes and counselors have high student ratios. Even though counselors and teachers want to spend more time with an individual student, they are often limited in what they can do in a brief period of time. Too often, counselors and teachers are perceived as people who are unavailable, uninterested, or too busy. Some students feel too great a personal distance between themselves and adults who could help. Many students turn to their peers when they are in need of help.

Too many well-intended adults have a narrow view of the concerns and problems that effect young people. Too many adults are like those found in the *Land of the Berry-Hoppers*.

## The Land of the Berry-Hoppers

Once upon a time, in a land not so far away, there was a remote and little known place called "The Land of Berry-Hoppers." It was a strange land divided by a dark bottomless river with unpredictable currents. On one side was a beautiful hillside with many tall berry-laden trees. Colorful leaves sparkled in the sunlight and gave the area its name—The Rainbow Forest. It was a dreamland filled with riches; yet, it was difficult to get there because the forest was only accessible by crossing the raging river.

On the other side of the river was a more desolate area, not so beautiful and lush with colors. There were no tall trees, only small bushes and shrubs without berries. And, it was in this Region of Preparation that the berry-hoppers were born and grew up.

Berry-hoppers were odd little creatures, with round furry bodies, long narrow feet, and two large light green eyes. From the time they were born, they were told about all the marvelous trees and berries in the Rainbow Forest. It was supposed to be a wonderful place to live, full of opportunity and security. It offered excitement and adventure. But, it was only for adult hoppers who had successfully learned their "berry" lessons and who had swam across the river.

In the Region of Preparation, the young-hoppers practiced branch bouncing, bark clinging, berry balancing, leaf springing, and, of course, basic berry bisecting. All of these skills would be useful when the reached the Rainbow Forest. They were told by their elders that they needed these skills and information in order to climb the trees and reach the highest levels where the most succulent berries were grouped.

Old Jake, a wise old hopper and teacher, often exclaimed, "You will never be a successful climber and have happiness unless you learn your lessons well. It's not always easy to be a berry-hopper in the Rainbow Forest, even though there are lots of wonderful things there." He and his friends frequently chided the young ones to pay attention, study their lessons, do their homework and prepare for the future.

Many of the young hoppers were excited when they listened to Old Jake talk about the Rainbow Forest. They looked forward to the day when they could seek out the high trees and use large baskets to collect a bountiful supply of juicy berries. Others were more skeptical, though they studied their lessons dutifully.

As you might know, berry-hoppers measured their time in the number of round moons that appeared in the sky. Young hoppers looked forward to when they would be 250 round moons old. This was a special time in their lives. They would hop to the river and start their swim to the Rainbow Forest, fully-prepared to reap the pleasures that were there.

However, the bottomless river was very wide. Sometimes the hidden currents swallowed the young-hoppers as they attempted the crossing. Natually, some hoppers were better swimmers and seemed to cross without much effort. Some had a much more difficult time, struggling with all their might to reach the other side. In fact, a few were taken by the current and never seen again. Others started, but turned back after wading into the river and feeling it's cold currents rushing downstream.

There were still others who repeatedly looked at the river and turned away without even trying. No amount of teasing, threats, or encouragement made a difference with these struggling berry-hoppers. The fear of being lost in the bottomless river was overwhelming. So, they contented themselves by practicing more branch bouncing, bark clinging, and basic berry bisecting, even though there were no berries to be found in the Region of Preparation.

One round moon, a few adult hoppers expressed their concern that too many young ones were failing to reach the Rainbow Forest. Something needed to be done to give them the courage to try the crossing. Apparently, they needed more help and preparation than what they were receiving. What good did it do for young hoppers to learn so many berry skills when they never reached the Rainbow Forest?

Eventually, young berry hoppers were also taught swimming and other survival skills which would help them cross the river. These skills were viewed as important as any others, for without them the other skills were meaningless. In addition, the young hoppers began to realize that if they all worked together and helped each other, then they could all enjoy the Rainbow Forest. There was a new joy in the Region of Preparation as the little hoppers went about the task of learning their lessons. They were all going to the Rainbow Forest someday.

## Meeting the challenges

Like the bottomless river with its raging currents, our swiftly changing society can be a fearsome force for many young people. Unfortunately, too many teachers and parents appear like Old Jake to their children— promising, pleading, pushing, and threatening when the crossing becomes difficult.

It's not easy for young people to cross over into adulthood in these times. It takes more than information and knowledge of math, science, language arts, and computer technology. If young students are to successfully negotiate the hidden currents and barriers that confront them along the way, then they must also help each other to meet the challenges and to learn coping skills. There can be little doubt that interpersonal and problem-solving skills are as essential to young people today as swimming was to the young berry-hoppers.

How can these skills be taught to children? They could be taught as most other subjects—through textbooks, workbooks, and classroom demonstrations. Or, they might be modeled by skillful adults. Hypothetical situations could be outlined and children could relate how they would resolve a problem, make a decision, or interact in a situation. While all of these have their place and can be useful, children learn best by doing. They need to experience the skills, to study and practice them. They need to integrate these skills into an effective pattern that makes sense to them, by using them in their everyday lives.

One of the most innovative and successful ways of teaching students coping skills and the value of interpersonal relationships is to design programs and projects where they are trained to facilitate personal and academic growth.

**What This Book Is About**

This book is the first of its kind. It is an attempt to provide suggestions and a format for building a *comprehensive student facilitator program* in an elementary or middle school. It presents seven steps that might be taken along the way (See Table 1.1). These steps are discussed in the chapters that follow.

More specifically, Chapter II helps you gain an understanding of how children have been helpers to one another for many years. Early attempts in the helping process are also described. This chapter can be of particular value when you build a case for your program. In Chapter III the first step toward building a program is examined. Some initial concepts and skills to be taught and the role of trainer or coordinator are outlined. Chapter IV will help you get organized. It takes you through the next three steps of building a program—forming a plan, enlisting support, and selecting student facilitators.

Twenty training sessions are described in Chapter V. These training sessions provide some experiences for facilitators at three different levels: beginning, intermediate, and advanced.

Helping projects are the goal of students in training. Different kinds of projects are presented in Chapter VI and these are related to four helping roles. All of these roles are part of being a "friendly helper." This chapter also provides some helpful hints for supervising facilitators.

In Chapter VII several methods for assessing and evaluating student progress are discussed. Some can also be used to help evaluate the progress of a program itself. Finally, the last chapter gives attention to the trainer as both facilitator and learner.

The companion book, *Becoming a Friendly Helper*, is specifically designed for the student facilitators in your program. Although it is possible to design a program without student books, they were carefully prepared to complement the ideas in this book.

It's an exciting journey along the seven steps. But first, let's look at how children have helped children.

**Table 1.1**
**Steps to a Comprehensive Facilitator Program**

Step 1: Making a Commitment (Chapter III)
Step 2: Forming a Plan (Chapter IV)
Step 3: Enlisting Support (Chapter IV)
Step 4: Selecting Student Facilitators (Chapter IV)
Step 5: Training the Facilitators (Chapter V)
Step 6: Implementing and Supervising Projects (Chapter VI)
Step 7: Assessing and Evaluating Progress (Chapter VII)

# Chapter II
# Children as Helpers

## Early Roots in Education

In a mountain region of India many years ago, a little Hindu boy named Sari lived in an orphanage. He was ten years old, but he described himself as "almost eleven." Sari was a good student, although he sometimes had problems with boys who liked to pick fights. He received high marks for his school work. Though often dirty and scratched, he was easily recognized for his bright smile which revealed ivory white teeth.

One early morning Sari's smile was especially noticeable. On his daily journey to fetch water from the river, he thought about his teacher's comments to him the day before. Sari learned that he was going to be a teacher's helper in an experiment.

As Sari climbed the path from the river, his pace picked-up, even though his water jug was quite heavy. He was anxious to meet with the other pupils who had also been chosen for this new assignment. Waiting in the shade of the banyan tree, each pupil wondered aloud about the nature of the experiment. They grew silent when the "head teacher" approached.

The teacher explained that all of them would be special leaders in the school and would henceforth be called "monitors." Each morning, student monitors would meet with teachers at the school and receive the day's lesson plans, along with some directions for teaching other students. Sari would be responsible for ten pupils. He would instruct and supervise them.

As Sari listened to this news, his mouth fell open in surprise. He had never known students his age to be given such important responsibilities. He felt proud that such a great honor had been bestowed upon him and he was determined to prove himself worthy.

The year was 1791 A.D. and the orphanage was attempting a very different approach in education. This monitorial style of instruction later became known as the "Bell-Lancaster" method.

## The Bell-Lancaster Method

The Bell-Lancaster method was used extensively between 1800 and 1850 in Europe and the United States. It became popular because of its efficiency and effectiveness in teaching children. Proponents of the system emphasized that student behavior improved in helpers and helpees. Education for children of poor families became economically possible. In addition, it placed more responsibility and trust in older students and provided them with leadership experiences. By supplementing teachers with high-performing students, individual instruction finally became possible for all students.

There were several variations of the method. One teacher, for example, instructed a group of fifty "monitors" who, in turn, each instructed and "drilled" ten other students. Thus, this teacher was able to reach and be responsible for 500 students. In another instance, an eleven year old boy and his assistants were in charge of an entire school of 300 students (Allen, 1976).

Though this method attained high acclaim for more than 50 years, it began to wane in the middle 1800s. First, teachers were not adequately trained in how to use children as helpers. They relied upon existing peer relationships without trying to improve them. Strict order and a formal structure provided little room for spontanaiety. Students were taught as they had been taught. Second, the system became associated with "cheap" education. Yet, without such a system, it would have been almost impossible to educate the poor. Wealthy families, on the other hand, provided individualized instruction for their children, and often employed their own adult tutors.

Third, the number of professional educators began to increase. They valued their training and certification. They also wanted to assume more responsibility for the education of young people and they became more critical of approaches which relied upon people without professional training and preparation. Ironically, this trend toward more professionalism also discouraged the use of students as an educational resource and dealt a damaging blow to an innovative approach to education.

## Cross-age Tutoring

Before large urban centers developed, the one-room school house was a landmark in most areas of the United States. Teachers were hired to instruct the children of a community and they all met together, regardless of age, in the same room. In these multi-age level classrooms, cross-age tutoring developed and became another historical step in education where children helped children.

It was not uncommon in these schools to select older students, who had mastered their lessons, to work with younger students who were just beginning the lessons. This cross-age tutoring was usually one-to-one, with about a two-year age difference between tutors and tutees. Children in helper roles were found to be useful assistants and to benefit from the experience (Devin-Sheehan, Feldman & Allen, 1976).

As the population grew and as more schools consolidated, larger schools with more teachers developed. This enabled educators to separate students into grade level classrooms. Though some teachers continued to use students as tutors within the same classroom, cross-age tutoring lost its appeal. Its prominence declined as an educational approach, much like the Bell-Lancaster method.

There are still one-room schools left in some rural areas of the United States. Devin-Sheehan, Feldman and Allen (1976) surveyed 110 one-teacher schools in Nebraska and learned that 56 percent used children in some kind of cross-age tutoring program. He also noted that the students who were tutored felt positive about the experience.

Perhaps unknown to educators who discouraged the use of monitoring and cross-age tutoring, there were some important benefits that fell to the students. Student helpers were given some special responsibilities which encouraged feelings of self-respect and self-worth. They felt important and trusted. Most took their responsibilities seriously. Teaching others something that they had already learned helped reinforce that learning.

The tutors also identified gaps in their own understanding. Such practice and application of the "lessons" helped them become more familiar with the ideas and concepts than they might have otherwise been. During the process, tutors also learned that helping others could be personally beneficial and rewarding to themselves.

The idea of children helping children has some strong historical roots in education. It is an important concept that does not need to be reborn as much as it needs rennovation and rethinking. The ways in which students work with other students as helpers need to be reorganized and adapted. Systematic training and preparation of the helpers needs to be carefully implemented. With this kind of attention, there are many important roles that students can play in the helping process.

## Students in Helping Roles

Although children can work in many helping roles, most can be categorized into one of four groups: student assistants, tutors, special friends, and small group leaders. Let's examine these.

### Student Assistants

As student assistants, children work primarily with school staff as they carry out their specific responsibilities. Student assistants usually help other students indirectly by their timely assistance to staff. Some teachers, for example, might have their assistants grade papers, carry messages to the office, pass out materials or help construct a bulletin board. Student assistants may work in the front office or library where they file papers and books, answer the telephone and take messages. Others may assist custodians in their tasks, perhaps picking-up and sweeping classrooms, moving equipment, or cleaning boards after school. Still others might be members of a safety patrol, a common group of helpers in most schools.

Safety patrol members usually work more directly with students, but they are still viewed as assistants because of the nature of their assignments. Patrol students primarily help in the supervision of children as they walk to and from school. On occasion patrols may serve as "monitors" in a hallway or at a school assembly. In most schools, however, patrols are given responsibilities that require interpersonal skills but they receive little or no training. Rashbaum-Selig (1976) described the traditional role or safety patrols as "directing younger children across streets and making sure that safety and traffic rules are obeyed." Patrols usually depend upon an authoritarian aproach in their work because they are not trained to be friendly helpers. They become an "arm of discipline and control" in the school and this can cause them conflicts with peers.

Although students have been assitants to school staffs in many ways, a review of the professional literature for the past ten years reveals only one article referring specifically to the student assistant role (Rashbaum-Selig, 1976). Yet, the continued use of student assistants, despite the lack of research and study, indicates that some benefits are being observed by school personnel.

When student assistants have no contact with other students or the public, perhaps there is no need for training in interpersonal skills. However, when they talk and work with others directly, then it behooves the staff to make sure that student assistants are given some systematic training in communication and relationship skills. This makes them an even more valuable resource.

**Student Tutors**

The number and variety of programs in which children tutor other children has been increasing (Gartner, Kohler, & Riessman, 1971). However, many of the current tutoring programs are quite different from earlier cross-age tutoring. One important trend is the addition of training the tutors for their roles (Melaragno, 1976).

Devin-Sheehan, Feldman, and Allen (1976) reviewed the professional literature on "children-tutoring-children" and examined the results and observations from more than 100 studies and articles. They criticized much of the research as lacking rigorous design, neglecting significant issues, and being generally inadequate in scope and procedures. Drawing from some of the more systematic research studies, they concluded that some tutoring programs can effectively improve academic performance of both tutees and tutors.

Allen and Feldman (1974) designed an experiment in which fifth graders, who were low-achievers in reading, tutored third grade students. The experimental group of fifth-graders voluntarily tutored some younger children while a control group studied alone. After two weeks, the tutoring group made significantly higher academic gains than the control group. It was concluded that tutoring improved the academic performance of the tutors.

Tutors across different grades and populations have been successful. For example, third graders (Circirelli, 1972) and fifth and sixth graders (Lakin, 1972) were found to be generally effective. More specific populations such as third grade low-achievers (Rogers, 1980) also proved helpful as tutors, as did retarded students (Wagner, 1973). Second and third grade high-achievers were also shown to be valuable tutors (Mollod, 1970). In fact, children as young as four years of age have had some degree of success in tutoring other children (Feshback and Devor, 1969). For the most part, there seems to be no significant differences among sex, race and socio-economic levels.

Tutors have worked with other children in almost every subject that is taught in the schools, including handwriting and alphabet recognition (Edwards, 1976), reading (Anderson, 1976; Melaragno, 1976; Norris and Wantland, 1972) and math (Cadiz, 1963). When older children tutored younger children with reading difficulties, the tutees gained 6 months in reading level while the tutors gained 3.4 years (Cloward, 1967).

Frager and Stein (1970) used high and low achieving students in sixth grade to tutor kindergarten children. As a result the children who received tutoring were superior in language readiness to a control group of children. Absenteeism was reduced. The tutors also benefitted as their attitudes toward school and attendance improved.

In the past, tutors were simply matched with other students and told, "Give him (or her) some help." This usually implied some coaching, additional instruction, clarification and practice. Sometimes the focus was entirely upon correction and evaluation. Practice sessions frequently became drills. More often than not, tutors tended to give most of their attention to subject matter when many times tutees also needed personal support and encouragement.

One of the most effective tutoring programs recorded in the literature described how fifth and sixth grade tutors were trained in using non-instructional conversation, appropriate use of praise, correction of incorrect responses, and elicitation of correct responses. Tutors tried to help kindergarten children improve their reading abilities. Reading scores improved significantly in favor of tutored children when compared with non-tutored children. (Niedermeyer, and Ellis, 1971).

Students who need the help of tutors are often those who have had persistent problems in their studies. They can be resistant. They frequently feel embarrassed or defensive when help is offered. Some tutees may even decline the help of a tutor because they fear that it labels them as "inferior" or "dumb." This is particularly evident in schools where tutors are only assigned to work with low-achievers. It is also present in those schools where tutors must rely on their natural instincts for teaching and being friendly helpers.

Without training and preparation in interpersonal and communication skills, the tutor role will likely be limited to that of a "task master." This is most unfortunate, especially since some teaching approaches (e.g. discovery method, language experience approaches) require students to discuss and explore ideas. A training program, in which they learn how to build helping relationships, can make tutors more effective and efficient.

## Students As Special Friends

When most adults are asked to think of a childhood friend, they find delight in the memories. Senior citizens, for example, often recall such memories in vivid detail. It seems that close friendships in childhood are remembered for a lifetime.

Relax for a moment and let your mind wander back into your own childhood years. Who comes to mind as you try to remember a close friend from your elementary school years? What characteristics do you recall most clearly? How old were you at the time? What was a fun thing you did together?

Special times with friends can be cherished childhood experiences. Close friends value one another and look forward to meeting and doing things together. They share experiences, thoughts, and feelings. They trust each other with personal secrets. When one is having some difficulties, the other tries to provide encouragement and support.

Some children feel left-out and lonely because they don't have close friends. Friendships are vital to the process of individual and social maturation. To become a fully-functioning adult, a person needs some positive interactions with "friends." These interactions provide practice in relating with others. They involve giving as well as receiving. They are full of joy and, at times, disappointment. But, they provide opportunities to express private needs, interests and desires.

Without friendships, children may withdraw and become isolated. Some develop inappropriate patterns of behavior to meet their personal needs of acceptance and recognition. The school bully and class clown are examples of children who are reaching out for attention and friendship in ineffective ways.

Teachers and parents know the value of children having friends. Some adults may worry about children who are socially isolated and coax them to get involved with other students. Some may attempt to "draw-out" these students by thrusting them into threatening situations, which only causes them to become shy, embarrassed and perhaps more socially withdrawn.

Other approaches have been used which are more productive. Among these are the buddy system, friendly guides, pen pals, and big brother/big sister programs. These roles are often talked about casually among professionals. Yet, they have received little attention in the professional literature. There are no studies or published discussions of them, except in passing or in some brief reference. But, they are roles in which children are helping children. Perhaps with more attention and some expanded functions, these roles, and others like them, could provide more opportunities for more student interaction. Let's look at these roles in more detail.

**Buddy System.** This method has been used by schools, summer camps, and community clubs to provide companionship for children. In a "buddy system," children are paired randomly or by preference in an attempt to gain more involvement and mutual responsibility.

For example, a playground supervisor noticed that four students frequently stood alone on the sidelines during recess. They usually watched others and were generally rejected when they attempted to play with other children. The supervisor responded by pairing the children and thus giving each of them a "buddy." The buddies then played such games as "throw and catch." The children were then given a list of questions to ask their buddies to become better acquainted. Later, the children met together and learned a game in which they all participated.

These four students were encouraged to get involved and to make new friends. Although there were times when they did not participate, withdrawal was no longer a consistant pattern. Each child began to have more positive experiences in relating to peers at recess.

In some summer camps, a buddy system is used in which a child becomes a guardian and monitor for a partner. Children keep track of their buddies and make sure they are nearby during activities such as hiking or swimming. In addition to helping with supervision, the system provides each child an opportunity to develop a close friendship. However, sometimes this imposed friendship works well and at other times it doesn't, depending upon the way in which the children respond to one another.

**Friendly Guides.** Sometimes new students in a school feel confused, scared, or on display, especially during their first few days. A teacher or counselor might assign a classmate as a friendly guide, someone who would greet and help orient an incoming student to the school. Such guides are often chosen because they are popular and are considered good role models. They can be trusted to escort new students around the school and "show them the ropes." These helpers usually introduce the new students to others and try to make them feel more comfortable. When teachers and counselors are busy, they provide a source of information about school rules and policies.

Sometimes a friendly guide will become a close friend to a new student. First acquaintances are in a position to foster a close relationship, at least more so than if left to chance meetings at recess or on the playground. On the other hand, sometimes friendly guides are not prepared to be friendly helpers.

For example, when Mark arrived at his new school he was assigned to Aron who showed him the school facilities. Aron was eager to tell Mark about the school and to show him which lessons in the books had been completed and which ones were currently being studied. At first, Mark welcomed his help, but later found Aron too demanding and possessive of his time. While Aron thought he was being helpful, Mark wondered if he had inherited an anchor more than a guide. Mark wanted to meet other students and be friends with more than just one person. Aron's well-intended actions did not provide the kind of friendship that Mark wanted and they soon became classroom acquaintances rather than close friends.

**Pen Pal Programs.** Another friendship experience provided in some schools is that of being a "pen pal." Through a pen pal program, children have the opportunity to become acquainted with someone whom they didn't know before.

Pen pal programs probably started with teachers who encouraged children to write students in foreign countries or other states. First, it is a practical writing experience and encourages students to use the writing skills they learn in school. Second, the exchange of letters provides students with more information about life in other regions. Pen pals write about events and customs in their community. But, they also include personal statements about themselves. This is particularly true after an exchange of several letters. In this sense, the letters provide an avenue for self-expression and are directed to someone who, because of distance, is non-threatening, accepting, and assumed to be understanding. Consequently, pen pals can become special friends and some continue to write each other for many years.

The authors know personally, for example, one woman who has been writing her pen pal for 17 years. It began when she was in the fourth grade and started writing a young girl in England. The two exchanged letters over the years, relating the special events of their lives, such as boy friends, vacations, graduations, marriages, and the death of a family member. Over the years, the letters grew more personal and perhaps provided an important sharing experience and catharsis that was satisfying to both.

One year, a surprise telephone call from England made a holiday season even more special and eventful. There is still talk and hope of someday meeting each other face to face. Their pen pal friendship has become a bonding and personally enriching experience. These two women provide dramatic testimony to the powerful impact that sharing with a special friend—even through the mail—can have on a person's life.

**Big Brothers/Big Sisters.** Young children "look up" to older students and adults. Their look is often one of wonder, admiration, envy, and respect. They frequently try to immitate or copy the behaviors of successful older persons whom they aspire to be like. They have heroes and form fan clubs. They collect posters, cards and other special effects of local and national celebrities.

Realizing this phenomena, teachers and counselors try to identify students whom they see as models for others. They try to put these students in positions where they can be examples. In addition, young children usually like the idea of having a "big brother or sister" who takes an interest in them.

The terms "Big Brother" and "Big Sister" gained nation-wide attention when adult service organizations in many communities wanted to do something for juvenile delinquents, especially those who lacked a stable family structure or who had no father at home. Assigned to be a "big brother," a man in a community service club might take a young boy out for lunch, on a fishing trip, or perhaps to a game. These efforts were apparently so successful that "Big Brother" programs became a popular project for many organizations. Similarly, "Big Sister" programs also developed.

In addition, these terms have been used on college campuses for many years, especially within the fraternity and sorority system. An older and more experienced student is assigned to help a "pledge" adjust to college and to develop study habits. The big brother or sister is also the confidential advisor of the new student. Assignments are usually made on the basis of similar interests and assumed compatibility.

Some high schools have assigned students to be big brothers and sisters to elementary school students (e.g. Winters & Arent, 1969; Vassos, 1971). The terms are appealing and perhaps helped the public become more receptive to the idea that older students could help younger students in a personal way, beyond just academic tutoring. There seems to be some evidence that these kinds of peer programs are widely spread in many states. Yet, published literature about them is limited. In addition, it is apparent that these programs matched students on interests and a willingness to help and be helped without emphasizing a systematic training and helping program.

The concept of "big people helping little people" as representative brothers and sisters is also attractive within elementary schools. Upper grade students can be assigned to help primary grade children.

The Big Friend" program in Mesa, Arizona (Baker, 1973) is part of the school curriculum. Opportunities are provided for two children to work together as a team in a one-to-one relationship. Older students, nine to thirteen years of age, team with a younger student (Little Friend), five to eight years of age, in an attempt to meet the needs of both members of the team. The program began out of concern that some older students (one was overweight, a second lacked feelings of self-worth, and a third was epilectic) needed some opportunities that would help them gain more self-confidence and some experiences that would require self-direction and leadership. Currently, there are several teams working together in the school.

The director of the Big Friend program prepares a schedule of times when teams may work together, arranges for a work space, and supervises the Big Friends. The supervisory sessions focus upon displaying and explaining use of materials, discussions with friends, making materials, and resolving partner problems. While there are some social gains as a result of the matched friends, it is a tutorial program and the primary emphasis is upon providing academic assistance.

Norris and Wantland (1972) described how "Big Brothers and Big Sisters" could assist younger schoolmates succeed in reading. While some personal gains might indirectly result from the matching of students (e.g. increase responsibility, cooperativeness, generosity, regular attendance at school, and feelings of success) this program was primarily directed to academic progress in reading, which was described as the ultimate goal of the program. No interpersonal skills training was provided. However, attention was given to matching the personalities of the students. Positive feedback on the program was obtained from the school counselor, physical education teacher, and classroom teachers.

## Students as Small Group Leaders

The professional literature is also sparse in reporting how children have helped other children by being small group discussion leaders. Yet, observation in schools suggests that students can and are providing valuable assistance in this helping role.

Though some classes in elementary schools may be small, most average between 25 and 35 students. In a few cases, teachers have been assigned as many as 50 students, with perhaps a teacher-aide to help them. Managing large groups of children is not new to teachers but the most effective teachers know the value of dividing a large group into smaller groups on occasion. They rely upon student leadership because it is impossible to be present in all the groups.

Some teachers use small group activities to help motivate their classes. They divide students into teams, which may be matched against one another in competition. In most cases, a team has a "captain" who is appointed by the teacher or selected by students. The captain helps coordinate the team's efforts.

In some instances, leadership in the group is rotated among students so that each has a turn at being captain. On other occasions, the group members decide who will be their leader. It is not uncommon, in these cases, for students to choose the "stars" of the class. These popular students can easily be identified by observation or on a sociogram. Unfortunately, there are a few students who are invariably picked last for teams and they are rarely chosen by their peers to be leaders or captains. Even when given an opportunity to be leaders by the teacher, these students often fail because they lack the necessary skills to give them self-confidence and help them succeed.

Physical education teachers commonly use student leaders in large and small group activities. For example, a student might take roll, lead exercises, check equipment out and in, demonstrate a skill, or "coach" others. Some classroom teachers have learned that students enjoy talking about their lessons in small groups and this increases involvement and participation in class. For instance, one teacher divided her class into small groups and each group selected a leader and a recorder. One group task was to identify characteristics of a "great" leader. In a math task, the group members thought of different ways that a particular concept is used in everyday life. In another group task a leader showed "flashcards" while students practiced multiplication tables.

When teachers use students as small group leaders, they frequently give them specific roles and tasks to perform. This may include reviewing instructions, initiating a discussion, giving permission to speak, recording key ideas, and presenting a review of the discussion to the class.

Counselors have also found it helpful to use small group leaders in their work. Some have appointed co-leaders for groups. A student co-leader may help the counselor in certain activities and discussions. Students who have experienced the group before, or who would personally benefit from the leadership experience, are usually chosen. Other times, counselors have incorporated some "booster" students in their groups as models for other children.

Hansen, Niland, and Zanti (1969) published a study of behavioral models in counseling groups. Counselors formed groups designed to promote social learning of students from low-sociometric families. They found that the learning process of the groups was enhanced when a few model students were included.

Surprisingly, the number of teachers and counselors who are using small group leaders to help them in their work is limited. Moreover, it is usually the "stars" who are given the leadership opportunities. Adults often look for students who can take charge, someone to whom they can delegate responsibilities. Without a training program, they rely upon the "natural" leader.

Natural leaders, as they are called, have the kind of personality that enables them to relate well with their peers. Students look to them for direction and depend upon them to be supportive or lead them through a task. Even these leaders, however, feel uneasy at times with their roles and worry about their ability. They rely on what has worked for them in the past and the skills that they have accumulated from previous experiences. Without exception, these natural leaders could benefit from systematic training in interpersonal skills and most would use their training to full advantage.

Other students, with less polularity and fewer skills, are likely to feel more self-doubt and experience more anxiety when asked to be a group leader. They would especially benefit from a leadership program. Many would find the courage to try new ideas and assert themselves more in positive ways.

## Peer Facilitator Programs

The 1960s and 1970s were marked by turbulent times. There was an uprooting of traditional organizations and the structure of society. Rebellion against time-honored values swept the nation's schools and college campuses, as restless young people clamored for more human rights, more justice and more responsibility in decision-making. Communication gaps between young and old led to misunderstandings and angry confrontations. It was the beginning of the age of anxiety.

Toffler (1970) wrote about future shock and the effects of rapid change on society. Change was coming so fast that people felt disoriented and confused. Most people wanted to know more about what was happening in their lives and be more involved. Personal growth groups and self-help books became a sign of the times, as more and more people sought ways to cope with the fast pace of living.

There were not enough helpers who had the professional credentials to meet the needs of people. Increasing these services led to employment of more paraprofessionals. Finally, it seemed natural and easy to encourage students to help each other through peer counseling and peer facilitating programs. Many educators were surprised and encouraged that the programs met with so much success and acclaim.

## College and Secondary School Programs

The first peer facilitator or peer counselor programs for students began on the college and university campuses. Dormitory counselors and resident assistants had been a part of college life, but with additional training these upper class men and women could do more than patrol the halls or report infractions of school policies. Brown (1965) was among the first to report how college students could be trained as counselors and facilitators. Others followed (e.g. Zunker and Brown, 1966; Ettkin and Snyder, 1972; Simpson, Pate and Burks, 1973). Most of these programs, and others like them, focused primarily upon academic and social learning, orientation to college and dorm life, educational planning, and some "peer counseling."

Later, the peer counseling movement entered the secondary schools and received some extra momentum when it was associated as a way of encountering the drug culture, which was moving to high school campuses. Vriend (1969), for example, developed a program in an inter-city high school, using high-performing achievers as peer leaders. Group discussions were organized so that peers could interact on a more personal level. The program had a positive effect upon student grade point averages, attendance at school, and punctuality.

Hamburg and Varenhorst (1972) initiated a peer counseling program in the Palo Alto, California high schools that received national attention. It sparked the development of systematic training programs for young people who wanted to be peer counselors. Their work was followed by others who developed similar programs for high school students (e.g. Leibowitz and Rhodes, 1974; Sprinthall and Erickson, 1974; Samuels and Samuels, 1975; Gray and Tindall, 1978; Myrick and Erney, 1978 & 1979).

Although these peer counselors or facilitators may have participated in some familiar roles (e.g. student assistant, tutor, special friend, small group leader), there was an important difference. These programs prepared students for the helping roles and part of the preparation was an emphasis upon interpersonal and communication skills. In addition, trained peer helpers were encouraged to become more personally involved with their classmates and younger students in the schools. This peer facilitator or peer counseling movement in the secondary schools has met with much success and has still not reached its peak.

**Emergence of Elementary School Programs**

During the decades of the 1960s and 1970s, guidance in the schools was also marked by the emergence of a new kind of counselor. Beginning in the early 1960s, more counselors began to appear at the elementary school level. State and federal legislation, as well as school district support, contributed to their employment until there are, at this time, approximately 12,000 counselors in the elementary schools of the United States. Many more counselors are anticipated in the future.

Elementary school counselors believe in a developmental approach to counseling and guidance, although they also work with remedial and crisis situations. Because there is often only one counselor per school, regardless of the school population, counselors have had to rely more upon small and large group procedures. They work closely with teachers in classroom guidance activities or meet with groups of students in their guidance offices.

In addition, these counselors consult with teachers, parents and administrators. They also coordinate guidance services for the school, make referrals and work with district support staff. At times, it seems that their job responsibilities are endless and some tasks encroach upon their counseling time. Consequently, many counselors are now turning to peer facilitator programs as one solution to reaching more students and to providing a developmental guidance approach for all children in the school.

Following the lead of the peer programs established in colleges and high schools, elementary school counselors began exploring ways in which students could be trained in interpersonal skills so that they could be helpers to others. Several published guidance programs (e.g. Dinkmeyer (DUSO), 1970; Palomares (Magic Circle), 1970) were already emphasizing interpersonal skills through their affective education activities. Without too much more effort, some counselors began asking a few students to lead or to co-lead some of these effective educational activities in classrooms or small groups. The results were encouraging.

In addition, in some school districts high school students worked on projects in the elementary schools as tutors, special friends and small group leaders. In general, they were teacher and counselor assistants.

However, for some districts such projects presented a problem because the facilitators had to travel to and from their respective schools and because supervision was awkward. Sometimes it was difficult to coordinate times and schedules. At other times follow-up activities were delayed.

Some counselors and teachers in the elementary schools recognized these limitations and decided to develop their own peer helper programs. Cross-age tutoring, for example, had already proven to be effective within the elementary school. Why not some special friend and small group facilitator projects? By experimenting and through trial and error, more and more peer helper programs began to appear. It is impossible to estimate the number of such programs that have been started in the schools. However, more reports of peer or student facilitator programs have begun to appear in the literature.

**Some Successful Forerunners**

Kern and Kirby (1971) were among the first to research the effectiveness of trained peer helpers. They selected twelve fifth and sixth grade students who were rated favorably on a peer-rating inventory and were relatively free from adjustment problems. The students participated in three one-hour training sessions and were called "peer helpers."

The training consisted of three major phases: understanding behavior, changing behavior, and learning the role of peer helpers. Following an Adlerian model, peer helpers were taught to encourage positive behavior in other students. They learned to help the school counselor identify goals of misbehavior and to assist in explaining more effective ways of behaving to children with adjustment problems. As small group helpers they would try to make other members feel accepted. After training, teams of three peer helpers were assigned to groups of poorly adjusted fifth and sixth grade students and assisted the counselor with the group counseling.

A pre-test post-test control group design was used to investigate the effectiveness of the peer helpers in the groups. Kern and Kirby concluded from their findings that peers can be an important force when utilized in group counseling. An analysis of the pre- and post-test scores showed that teachers perceived the peer helper group to make higher gains on a behavior identification checklist than the control group or the counselor-oriented group. Other findings were less significant. However, based on their research, Kern and Kirby also concluded, "Peers can assist the counselor to work more effectively with children who have adjustment problems. Elementary school counselors may be overlooking a potent force by not utilizing peers in group counseling in a more systematic fashion."

Mosley (1972), speaking to the Florida state legislature in support of elementary school guidance and counseling, described a "cadet program" in which fifth and sixth grade students with social and/or academic needs were assigned to help primary grade children who needed "that little special touch afforded by a one-to-one relationship." The results were "gratifying and the cadets were filled with pride from their accomplishments with the younger students."

Wrenn and Mencke (1972) trained college students to be peer counselors. They also cited instances where elementary students facilitated the growth and development of other elementary school students. However, they did not report any specific descriptions or data.

In regard to student helping programs they reported that supervisors have control in applicant screening, student helpers gain internal motivation; helpees as well as helpers benefit from the experience; students take a responsible posture in their work; the process does not cause psychological harm; and supervisors become inspired and learn from the program. Although they focused upon secondary and college programs, it was obvious that these same statements of support were true for elementary school programs.

Briskin and Anderson (1973) reported a study of the effectiveness of sixth grade boys as contingency managers to disruptive third graders. Six boys were selected for the program from teacher recommendations. After six half-hour training sessions, they became "learning assistants" and participated in a behavior modification program designed to reduce the frequency of disruptive behaviors of two third grade boys.

To prepare the sixth graders for their roles in the program, training sessions focused on recognizing the target behaviors, administering a time out procedure when the target behaviors occurred, and giving positive reinforcement for appropriate behaviors.

After training, each of the assistants spent a half hour each day in the third grade classroom. When they observed one of the target behaviors, the time out procedure was implemented. The older student signaled the third grade boy to leave the room with him and both sat quietly for four minutes before returning to class. If no time outs or only one time out were used in the half-hour period, the learning assistnat gave the third grader a compliment as positive reinforcement.

This intervention continued for eighteen consecutive school days. At its conclusion, inappropriate behaviors were reduced in one student from 104 per hour to 1.2 and for the other student from 64 per hour to 0.7. The program had been successful. In addition, sixth grade teachers reported improvement and maturation of the students who participated as learning assistants.

McCann (1975) described a peer counseling program in which sixth grade students participated in eight one-hour training sessions. Listening skills, nonverbal communication, self-disclosure, reflective listening, and developing alternative courses of action when faced with a problem received attention.

Student helpers worked in a school "drop-in center" which was open to fifth and sixth grade students during recess or lunch two days a week. At least one peer counselor was scheduled in the center, waiting for students to come and discuss their difficulties or concerns. As a result, students' attitudes toward mental health in the school were enhanced. It was reported that student awareness of helping techniques increased and that peer counselors enjoyed the experience.

Kum and Gal (1976) cited a program in which sixth grade students were trained as peer helpers to assist other students with "minor concerns." They were trained for ten one-hour sessions, built around constructive communication and decision-making skills. According to the student trainees' reponses on a post-training questionnaire, the program improved their attitudes toward school, improved their relationships with teachers, and others and enhanced self-understanding.

Gumaer (1973) introduced the term "peer-facilitator" into the literature. He described a program which taught fifth grade students to clarify, reflect, and give feedback. After training, they became leaders to small groups of second grade students.

Students were selected for training on the basis of school records, observations, consultations with teachers, and the results from a sociogram. Eight students who appeared to be leaders participated. In the first training session, some group activities helped the students to become better acquainted. Guidelines for discussion were given and the definition of a leader was explored. In the second session, students learned about "facilitative responses."

Listening was discussed during the third session. Students practiced listening and responding to each other's statements. In the fourth session, they were introduced to "effective feedback" procedures and they practiced giving feedback to each other in triads. The fifth and sixth sessions were used for review. Later, a few sessions dealt with some additional topics such as majority and minority groups, stereotypes, and prejudice. After training, the peer facilitators led small group discussions in the second grade classroom. The topics presented were essentially the same as those experienced by the facilitators in training.

In 1975, Gumaer investigated the effects of a peer facilitator training (PFT) program and group leadership experience on low performing elementary school students. The study examined eight hypotheses regarding personal, social and emotional adjustment of students. Sixty-four low performing fifth grade students were randomly selected from four schools. In each school, eight low performing students were assigned to an experimental group and eight served as controls. The experiment lasted a total of eight weeks.

During the first week, student subjects, teachers, and counselors completed pre-experimental measures. The next three weeks included the PFT program which consisted of group training sessions where trainees learned self-disclosing and group facilitator skills. During the fifth through seventh weeks, trained peer facilitators led small group discussions in third grade classrooms. These discussions took place twice a week for the three weeks and lasted approximately twenty minutes each. Following the peer-led discussions, the peer facilitators and their respective counselors met for supervison.

Although there was a positive trend, no significant differences were found between the experimental and control groups. Teachers, administrators and students offered positive statements and felt encouraged. In addition to its being one of the most controlled reserach studies of peer facilitators, it focused upon the training of low-performing students in hope that such training would be "treatment." Gumaer later described the PFT model in other professional publications (1976 ; 1980).

The acronym "H.E.L.P.I.N.G." was used by Keat (1976) to descibed the components of a multimodal treatment approach for training peers. Included were Help, Empathy, Learn, Peers-people-personal problems, Image-interests, Needs, and Guidance of behaviors and consequenses. While he did not describe the details of a program, he encouraged trainers to consider these training concepts.

Anderson (1976) reviewed the history and issues related to peer facilitators in the elementary schools. He credited the emergence of such programs to the success of counselors who turned to paraprofessionals for help and to the successful use of high school and college students as peer counselors.

A "Student Helper Program" in Tempe, Arizona, was described by Edwards (1976). Students were trained in groups of eight. Each group had different training procedures, depending upon selected projects. For example, one group learned instructional techniques of teaching math to younger children. Student trainees received a folder of useful materials and kept a log of their helpees' progress. This provided an on-going evaluation. Other student trainees learned to assist with "social needs." The counselor and helper designed a planned intervention to meet the needs of each child who worked with the student helpers. She reported that students, teachers, and parents strongly supported the program.

Jacobs, Masson, and Vass (1976) encouraged more widespread use of peer helpers. They offered several suggestions about implementing programs. Among their recommendations were: gain administrative support, select student helpers carefully, and use a training model similar to McCann's work (1975). It was also suggested that a beginning peer facilitator program should start small and expand later. They concluded that trained peer helpers can be of assistance with student orientation, minor academic problems and with students who need to talk with someone about themselves.

As editor of the *Elementary School Guidance and Counseling Journal*, Myrick (1976) supported and recommended elementary school peer facilitator programs. He suggested that peer facilitators "may be the only viable approach for providing guidance services to all children" and "... helping children to help other children is one kind of counselor intervention that should be included in all elementary school guidance programs."

A program which trained fourth grade students to be group leaders with second grade students was described by Weise (1976). Students were selected for the training program on the basis of leadership ability, peer respect, self-expression, and ability to express feelings. In general, trainess learned the facilitative skills of questioning, listening, and reflecting feelings. The facilitators led discussions with small groups of second grade students using some published guidance materials (e.g. DUSO, Magic Circle, and Focus On Self-Development). Weise reported a closeness and pleasure in watching the peer facilitators' personal growth.

Hoffman (1976) trained some peer "models" before they participated in groups with other students. These models were chosen on the basis of their leadership abilities, as seen by the counselor in informal settings around the school. Those chosen received ten sessions of training in feelings, listening, and confronting. After training, they were placed into all boy or girl groups with students who had been identified as being verbally or physically agressive or withdrawn. Comments from parents, teachers, and participants suggested positive attitudinal and behavioral changes, with both student models and with group participants.

Can children as young as ten years of age respond favorably to training in empathic skills? Vogelsong (1978) found that fifth grade children, who recieved training, showed greater improvement in empathic skills than a control group. Training focused on nonverbal expression, recognition of emotion, showing empathic acceptance, giving empathic responses, and the importance of being aware of one's own feelings. The results of his study suggested that "not just knowledge and not just experience, but active, specific, concrete skill training can become a significant part of affective education even in the elementary grades."

Rockwell and Dustin (1979) developed another model for training peer counselors. They recommended the following goals: 1) to increase counseling effectiveness; 2) to increase the visibility of the counseling program; 3) to increase the amount of counseling within the school; and 4) to facilitate psychological growth within the trainees. They also recommended using self-selection, faculty and student nominations, counselor recommendations, and some objective criteria for student selection. Content of the training sessions might include how to make referrals, procedures in the counseling office, communication skills, self-awareness, and group techniques. They concluded that each peer helper program should be tailored to the particular setting.

Mastroianni and Dinkmeyer (1980) reported a program which included ten half-hour training sessions. Fifth graders were selected for training on the basis that they were willing to devote the time for training and had an interest in helping other students. The sessions focused upon: (1) Getting acquainted; (2) Listening and recognizing strengths; (3) Listening and developing trust; (4) Reflective listening; (5) Exploring alternatives; (6) Reviewing facilitative skills and role-play; (7) I-messages and providing choices; (8) Public interview and demonstration; and (9) & 10) Practicing group leadership skills. They concluded that a peer facilitator program can provide an opportunity for students ". . . to gain confidence and abilities and thus learn to feel significant in socially useful ways."

Bowman and Myrick (1980) described a facilitator program which trained students from grades 3-6 to become "Junior Counselors." Some students were selected on the basis that they were well-adjusted in school, while others were chosen because they had some difficulties. Fourteen training sessions, lasting about 45 mintues each, followed seven phases: (1) Getting started; (2) Nature of helping; (3) Feelings; (4) Listening; (5) Helping responses; (6) Problem-solving; and (7) Things to remember.

Students were assessed on their skills and knowledge of helping concepts before they began various projects. In one project, students helped fourth grade teachers talk about some of their classroom concerns. Using the Piers-Harris Children's Self-concept Scale, all the facilitators showed positive gains from pre- to post-evaluations.

Peer faclitator programs are in existence in many schools across the country. Some are still at an experimental stage. Others have started, floundered, and disappeared. Still others have been more selective in their tasks and projects, thus cautiously moving toward a more comprehensive approach.

There are many programs that could not be reported here because they have not been described in the literature. Nevertheless, observations and reports from conferences and professional meetings indicate that there is a need for more training programs that use a systematic approach. In most facilitator programs, it has been school counselors who have been coordinators. However, it is also feasible that teachers and administrators could become more involved in the training process.

## Students as Helpers: Some Benefits

When students are involved in the helping process, observers tend to conclude that the experience is postive and productive. Adults like seeing young people help each other. Some even view it as cute and find it charming. But, if the programs are to be valued as an educational approach and are to be incorporated into even more schools, then there must be more substantial proof beyond testimonials that such programs have some benefits.

A review of the professional literature within the last ten years indicates that students have assisted other students to improve in the areas of 1) academic performance; 2) attitudes about self, others and school; 3) socially acceptable behaviors; 4) personal helping skills; and 5) coping skills. Although these categories are frequently interrelated and not exclusive to any one study, they provide a framework for examining some of the contributions that students have made when working with their peers.

**Academic Performance.** Recent surveys have indicated there is a trend for students to graduate from high schools with lower levels of achievement in subject areas such as reading, math and science.

Facilitator programs offer an exciting and practical strategy which can help increase academic gains. Several studies, for example, have reported programs where children help other children learn and participating students have raised their academic performance significantly (e.g. Anderson, 1976; Edwards, 1976; Melaragno, 1976: Myrick, 1976; Norris and Wantland, 1972).

**Attitudes About Self, Others and School.** Developing a healthy attitude toward one's self, others, and school sometimes requires special attention. It seems that students who view themselves, others, and school negatively perform poorly in their classes and relate inappropriately with others. They provide a negative influence. These students often respond by rebelling or withdrawing from school activities and tasks.

Student facilitator programs offer an opportunity for these students to have interesting and positive school experiences (e.g. Bowman and Myrick, 1980; Gumaer, 1973; Hoffman, 1976; McCann, Gartner, Kohler, and Riessman, 1971).

**Socially Acceptable Behaviors.** Student facilitators can have a positive effect upon socially acceptable student behaviors (Baker, 1973; Gumaer, 1973; Kern and Kirby, 1971; Rashbaum-Selig, 1976). Students learning to be facilitators discuss and explore relationships. They also think about the behaviors that are effective and ineffective with people.

In some cases, a target student might be a part of the facilitator group and training becomes treatment. This concept has been used effectively with students who need special attention because of disruptive behaviors (e.g. Gumaer, 1975; Bowman and Myrick, 1980).

**Personal Helping Skills.** In a student facilitator program, a student acquires a basic understanding of helping skills. After training, the students can be more effective with others. Because student facilitators are "where the action is," they are often the first source of help to which students might turn. They are within the context of where problems first surface. Teachers and counselors, on the other hand, sometimes don't learn of problems until they have already become intense and erupted. At that time, they are more difficult to resolve and take more time.

Teachers, counselors and librarians have found student facilitators to be valuable helping resources in school. As assistants, they augment the delivery of school services to all students (Gartner, Kohler & Riessman, 1971; Gumaer, 1976; Jacobs Masson, & Vass, 1976; Melaragno, 1976; Weise, 1976).

**Coping Skills.** Facilitator programs have, as a central focus in training, many skills and concepts which help individuals cope with the changing world around them. For example, students can learn listening and communication skills, decision-making and problem-solving skills. In the process, they learn to be more responsible for their actions (e.g. Baker, 1973; Edwards, 1976; Hoffman, 1976; Keat, 1976).

## Professional Support

The American School Counselor Assocation, the largest professional organization of school counselors at all levels, has embraced the concept of peer counseling for the secondary schools and provided a position statement in support of it (*ASCA Newsletter*, 1979). There is an emphasis upon increasing the effectiveness of counseling and guidance programs by training students to help other students. Such an "outreach" program is viewed as expanding guidance services.

This position statement concludes:

> It is imperative that all Guidance and Counseling Departments in the school plan, initiate and implement a peer counseling program. Well-trained peer counselors can have a positive effect on students that no one else can provide. Students sometimes relate and accept alternative patterns of behavior from peers who are struggling with similar feelings and problems. Peer counselors can create a tremendous positive impact on the student population.

Since that time counselors and counselor educators have realized that the same needs and benefits are also true for elementary and middle schools. Moreover, young students can learn many helping concepts and skills as easily as their older peers. They can engage in some of the same roles and perform some of the same functions. Children can help children in the same way that adolescents can help adolescents, and adults can help adults.

## Chapter III
# Beginning a Student Facilitator Program

Every peer or student facilitator program is unique. Each has its own characteristics that are affected by the students and professional personnel that are involved. Each has its own organization and training emphasis, which in turn determines the student projects that can be successfully implemented. Each creates its own potential in the face of siutational limitations and each develops its own identity. Participating students and program coordinators often conclude: "Our group is really special. There's nobody like us."

Your student facilitator program will have it's own uniqueness and identity. It will be a reflection of your personality and interests, as well as those of your students and supporting staff. Yet, there are some common characteristics that often make successful programs. This chapter gives attention to those similarities. It will help you look at some important issues and sequential steps that are a part of building an effective and rewarding program.

Your program may be just beginning. Or, you may already have an established program and are looking for some more ideas. Regardless, there are some basic considerations that eventually confront a program coordinator or leader. Among these are: What is the purpose of your program? What concepts and skills will be taught to students? How will facilitators use their skills with others? How will you know if your program is successful or not?

The answers to these and other questions will determine your success. They can also help you conceptualize what you want for your school.

There are many ways to build a program. However, there are seven steps that you can take along the way:

Step
  1: Making a Commitment

Step
  2: Forming a Plan

Step
  3: Enlisting Support

Step
  4: Selecting Student Failitators

Step
  5: Training the Facilitators

Step
  6: Implementing and Supervising Projects

Step
  7: Assessing and Evaluating Progress

Related to each of these sequential steps are some important questions. Together they might be viewed as a set of guidelines or a checklist. The remainder of this book gives attention to these steps, questions, and some answers. Let's get started by looking at step 1 in this chapter.

## Step 1: Making a Commitment

You will want to avoid developing your program in a haphazard and unsystematic manner. In some cases, where this has happened, counselors and teachers have experienced less success and, more often that not, these programs were discontinued after a short experimental period.

Historically, we know that children have helped children. They continue to do so even today. Yet, few attempts have been made to organize this helping process so that maximum benefits can be obtained. So much learning potential is lost when student help is taken for granted or not used. As more organized peer and student facilitator programs develop, we will realize more than ever before the advantages that students, teachers, counselors, and parents receive.

Making a commitment is an important first step in developing a program. But what do you need to know before that can be done? You might begin by first examining the need and purpose of the program and some possible objectives. You will also want to consider the concepts and skills to be taught facilitators. This will help clarify your own interests and decisions. While still other factors may influence your final commitment, some basic considerations provide a starting place.

## The Need for the Program

Is there a need for a program? Chapter I outlined many of the problems facing young people as they grow to adulthood. They are facing different stresses and problems than most adults did when they were in school. There are more options and more choices to be made, and more models to draw upon. Everything is moving faster, including communication and transportation. It's a confusing world, at times. Non-specific anxiety is higher than it once was and the pressures of living in today's world have caused more family and individual stress.

In addition to the data presented in the first chapter, more could be added to emphasize the need for programs that help students learn more about themselves and how to cope with the problems that confront them. You may have access to supporting data that is specific to your own state, area or community and this would help dramatize the need for a program.

In addition, you may want to investigate the special needs of the children in your school or agency. In this way, you can both substantiate the need for your program and provide more specific projects to help meet those needs.

You might, for example, develop a brief questionnaire that could be administered to students in all grades. Students could check areas in which they would like more help.

It could ask them to describe problems that they see themselves and others facing as part of their school day. Many counselors do this routinely as part of their job and the information may already be available. In addition, teachers and principals might complete a survey which would help identify problem areas that need attention if students are to get along and learn more effectively. Likewise, parents can be involved, perhaps through parent-advisory groups.

The kinds of questions and information on a survey or questionnaire form will depend upon the interests, needs, and limitations that face a particular group of teachers, counselors, parents, and administrators. Unfortunately, there will be a few who don't want to survey people for fear that some small but vocal group in the community will perceive their efforts as non-academic or too intrusive. Most, however, recognize that a child learns all the time and from many sources. The purposes of a student facilitator program are very compatible with a school's mission.

## The Purpose of the Program

One of the first questions that you are likely to encounter from others is: "What are you trying to accomplish?" Or, "What's the purpose of your program?" Your answer may determine the kind of understanding and support you recieve.

Pehaps the ultimate purpose of any facilitator program is to enhance student learning, both personally and academically. In this sense, a program directly benefits: 1) students who learn to be facilitators; 2) students who work with the facilitators, either individually or in groups; and 3) the school staff who are responsible for helping all students to learn more.

**To Teach Communication and Coping Skills.** One purpose of a student facilitator program is to teach some communication and coping skills to students who are learning to be facilitators. They learn these skills so that they can be "friendly helpers" and better leaders. In preparing to be facilitators, and through projects where they work with others, they learn more about themselves and how these skills apply in their own lives. They learn to think about their own behaviors, attitudes, needs, interests, and rights; as well as those of others. In the process, students increase in self-confidence and self-respect.

**To Provide Learning Opportunities.** Another purpose is to provide opportunities for students to explore their thoughts and feelings with trained facilitators and to engage in some unique learning opportunities. Students who work with and receive help from facilitators can talk about their successes and their concerns. They can talk about what they like and dislike. They can discuss what they are learning in school and how it applies to them. For some, it is an opportunity to practice skills that they have learned. For others, it is a chance to discover and to investigate little problems that annoy them and distract them from their studies. This kind of interaction among students helps them to become more involved in the learning process—regardless of the subject area.

**To Improve Peer Relationships.** Because peer relationships are improved through student interaction that involves facilitators, everyone learns better and the school becomes a more enjoyable and encouraging place to be. Peer relationships affect the learning environment and positive experiences are essential for personal and academic growth.

**To Increase Responsible Decision-Making.** Still another purpose is to help both facilitators and the students with whom they work to become more effective and responsible decision-makers. It is not enough to learn more about one's self or about the surrounding environment. There are always problems to be resolved, decisions to be made, and actions to be taken. With the help of facilitators, students can explore their situations, alternatives, and possible consequences. Then, through their experiences they can learn to be more responsible citizens.

**To Improve the School Learning Climate.** An important purpose of a student facilitator program is to make school a more intellectually stimulating and rewarding place to be. Because students become more involved in the learning process, school is more interesting. Learning is more personal and relevant. They have more opportunity to share their ideas and to react to the ideas of others. Incapacitating anxieties, fears and problems are decreased. Because students are more active in sharing ideas, resolving problems, exploring concepts, and because peer relationships are more positive, the school atmosphere is more productive.

**To Mobilize Human Resources.** Finally, another purpose of a student facilitator program is to mobilize more human resources within a school and to provide timely assistance to teachers, counselors, and administrators. As "friendly helpers," student facilitators become positive extensions of teachers and counselors, allowing more attention to be given to students and their needs. Sometimes teachers and counselors are thwarted because of limited time, high student ratios, or other demands. With the assistance of student facilitators, they can reach more children and their own work becomes more enjoyable and rewarding.

You may think of other purposes for a student facilitator program. You might want to word them differently or select some that are specific to your own needs and interests. However, it is often helpful if you outline your program according to general and specific objectives. In the process, the purpose of your program is clarified.

## The Program's Objectives

You can define goals and identify training procedures better when you have program objectives. Objectives provide a focal point. They help you set priorities. They also enable you to select appropriate materials, activities and skills to be taught. Objectives determine student projects. In addition, they provide a basis upon which to evaluate the results of your efforts and the impact of the program.

### General and Specific Objectives

It can be helpful to think in terms of general and specific objectives. *General objectives* describe the over-all intent of a program or activity, whereas *specific objectives* detail the desired behaviors that should result from a program or activity.

Imagine that you are talking with a group of parents at a school P.T.A. meeting. Someone asks, "But, what's the program about?" You might respond by saying, "There are a lot of things that we hope to accomplish, but the program is designed to help students improve their listening skills; make better decisions; and, increase their feelings of self-worth and confidence, among other things." In brief, you have outlined some general objectives or expectations.

A list of some general objectives for peer or student facilitator programs appears in Table 3.1. Note that some of the objectives (i.e. No. 1-8) focus upon goals for students who are learning to be facilitators. Yet, these same objectives could also apply to students who are receiving help from facilitators.

What if someone should ask, "But, how will you know if students have more self-confidence?" You might respond by saying, "Students will, for example, be able to list at least three personal strengths about themselves." Or, "After completing the program the student facilitators will be able to initiate a discussion with three other students." While neither of these behaviors are totally indicative of self-confidence, they provide some evidence of it.

**Table 3.1**

**Some General Objectives of A Facilitator Program**

I. To Enhance Student Development by Improving:
   1. communication skills
   2. interpersonal relationships among students
   3. skills in observing and problem-solving
   4. responsible decision-making
   5. group leadership skills
   6. feelings of self-worth and self-confidence
   7. positive attitudes toward self, others, school and community
   8. ability and appreciation for helping others

II. To Enhance the Learning Environment by Providing:
   9. timely assistance to faculty
   10. extended guidance services to all students
   11. opportunities for more students to talk about their feelings and ideas and to be listened to
   12. more situations in which students explore alternative behaviors, natural and logical consequences, and personal responsibility
   13. more systematic approaches that involved students as helpers in the learning process
   14. a developmental rather than crisis focus to problem-solving
   15. a source of personal assistance and help within the context of the learning environment
   16. more opportunities to practice life's learning and coping skills
   17. more situations in which students can gain positive recognition
   18. opportunities for students to practice interpersonal skills and develop positive relationships
   19. A learn by doing supervised experience

*Each general objective can have related specific objectives which clarify its meaning or illustrate its intent.* Below are some general objectives, each with a related specific objective. Can you think of some more specific objectives?

General Objective: To develop or improve listening skills

Specific Objective: After listening to a person talk for two minutes, the facilitator will be able to summarize two ideas to the satisfaction of the talker, that were expressed.

Specific Objective: Someone is talking, the student will be able to maintain eye contact for a minimum of one minute and identify one feeling that was expressed by the talker.

Specific Objective: Each student will be able to write a clarifying statement related to the content of what someone has expressed in a brief statement.

Some other examples of specific objectives may be found in Table 3.2.

Now, start by making a list of objectives for the students that you want to train to be facilitators. What do you want them to learn? What outcomes do you expect? If it helps, use Table 3.1. List some general objectives that appeal to you.

After completing your list of general objectives, rank order the list from top to bottom. This will help you identify your most important goals—the ones that are of particular interest to you. Can you think of at least two specific objectives for each general objective that you rated highest?

This simple process can help you gain a better understanding of your program's purposes and goals. It can also help you identify appropriate training activities and exercises.

Sometimes it can be helpful to write a brief, narrative description of your program, describing in one or two paragraphs the general intent of your efforts. You might include a list of objectives for a certain time period. Most administrators like to have such an outline on file for easy reference.

## Table 3.2

**Some Specfic Objectives for a Facilitator Program**

Students will be able to:

1. identify key ideas from a two minute story about someone.
2. identify a feeling word which describes the emotion as someone describes an experience.
3. list four helping characteristics.
4. respond to someone who is confused and use all five parts of the problem-solving model.
5. maintain eye contact during a conversation with another student for five minutes.
6. increase the number of completed classroom assignments.
7. increase the frequency of positive statements in a student group.
8. give facilitative feedback.
9. lead a group of six students in a classroom discussion.
10. differentiate between open and closed questions.
11. cite at least five ideas that are important to a student who is self-disclosing.
12. initiate a helping relationship with someone who is of different sex, race or culture.
13. differentiate between helpful and less helpful statements.
14. write two positive statements about one's self and two statements about a desired change.

## Important Concepts and Skills

Studies of counseling, therapy, teaching, social work and other helping services provide us with a lot of information about human behavior and helping relationships. There are many theoretical models and numerous skills and techniques that have been advocated by contributors in these professions. Moreover, within the past few decades the growth of knowledge in these areas has been particulary impressive. There is so much information and so many ideas that can be applied to helping people that, at times, it can be overwhelming and confusing—even to professionals.

What, then, should you teach young people about human behavior and helping theories? What do they need to know before they can facilitate others? What concepts and skills are essential to their work?

Children can help one another without studying psychology and knowing counseling and teaching theories. The historical roots of children helping children support this assumption.

Therefore, extensive knowledge of counseling theories and psychological concepts seem to be more important for trainers to know and work from than for children to study and understand. Yet, there are few basic psychological concepts and skills that can help young people to be better facilitators than they would otherwise be.

Observation and study indicate that there are three conceptual and skill areas that need attention in preparing students to be facilitators. These are: 1) What is a helping relationship? 2) What can a person say to "facilitate" others to think about feelings and ideas; and 3) What are some decision-making skills that lead to responsible action? Let's look at these in more detail.

## The Helping Relationship

Have you ever noticed how you enjoy being around some people more than others? No doubt, you have found it easier to be close friends with a few people and these friendships have a special quality.

Here are some statements that were over heard:

> I don't know how we grew to be such good friends... I guess we just hit-it-off from the beginning.

> As we got to know each other better, we've learned that we have a lot of things in common. Sharing ideas made us good friends.

Sometimes close relationships just seem to happen, without apparent reason. There is a spark, a kindred feeling, a sense of comfort, and a subtle awareness of an instant liking for one another. Some call it a mutual inclination, a special bond, but they struggle when asked to define their relationship in more precise terms. "It's just there—caring, trust, acceptance and understanding. That's what makes it special."

Helping relationships, like friendships, also have a special quality to them and are sometimes difficult to describe. However, among all the descriptions the words *caring, trust, acceptance,* and *understanding* are most likely to occur. While there may be other descriptors that are just as important and insightful, these four basic characteristics are worthy of study by your students and you will want to help them explore the meanings.

The theories of Carl Rogers (e.g. 1951, 1957, 1959, 1961 and 1962) first drew attention to the characteristics of a helping relationship. He assumed that if certain conditions existed in a helping relationship, then a positive process would be set into motion which would lead to beneficial changes in a person's personality and behavior. These conditions (i.e. unconditional positive regard, empathic understanding, and personal congruence) were not only necessary but sufficient in the therapeutic process.

The early contributions of Rogers led to a popular counseling theory, referred to as Client-Centered Therapy, but his work has since become accepted as directly relevant to any helping relationship. Perhaps most important, his theories eventually opened the door to more helpers.

## Some New Helpers

It was during 1960s that a shortage of counselors, therapists and personnel workers occurred. A demand for more helping services in schools and colleges, rehabilitation and employment centers, social and mental health agencies led to a concentrated effort to prepare more professional workers. Still, there were not enough helpers. Consequently, the idea of using support personnel gained momentum which has continued to the present. Variously called subprofessionals, paraprofessionals, lay counselors, aides, assistants, and technicians— among other titles—these new helpers provided a new pool of jobs, some new modes of helping others, and some new data about the helping relationship and the therapeutic process.

As more research took place, it became increasingly clear that paraprofessionals could function effectively with clients and, in some cases, were even more effective than experienced professionals (Carkhuff and Truax, 1965; Pierce, Carkhuff and Berenson, 1967). Success seemed to depend upon the ability to offer or create a set of core dimensions in the helping relationship. In addition, Carkhuff and Berenson (1967) claimed that the absence or presence of these conditions in a relationship determined whether or not it was facilitative or retarding. Thus, some relationships were described as more "nourishing" than others, and "for better or for worse."

The core dimensions that received the most support were empathic understanding, positive regard, and genuineness. There were others (e.g. appropriate self-discosure, spontaniety, warmth, confidence, openness, flexibility, committment) that were also identified as potent agents in the helping process, but received less empirical support.

Peer counseling and facilitator programs developed in the 1960s and 1970s. In the beginning, program coordinators and trainers deliberately selected students on the basis of their personalities, assuming that they would be able to offer or create the helping conditions without much training. Later, it was recognized that other students could also be helpers, providing that they received some advanced preparation for their roles.

More recently, four books appeared which described peer counseling or facilitator programs. All of them were written for use with adolescents in the secondary schools. The authors recommended that students could become better helpers by learning characteristics of a helping relationship.

Samuels and Samuels (1975) in their book, *Peer Counseling*, focused primarily upon the importance of communication skills and techniques, suggesting experiential activities for each of the fifteen training sessions. They emphasized the importance of "trust," saying that it was necessary before individuals would speak freely. While other helping characteristics may have been implied, only the condition of trust received special attention.

Gray and Tindall (1978) identified seven areas related to teaching communication skills and the helping process. Attending, empathy, summarizing, questioning and genuineness are most closely related to the characteristics first posited by Rogers and his colleagues. The others are more related to skills that, if effective, help create the helping relationship described by Rogers and other client-centered theorists.

Myrick and Erney (1978, 1979) emphasized the term "peer facilitator" in their work, believing that very few students could learn to "counsel" other students. However, it was assumed that all students could learn to "facilitate" other students, especially if they have received training in communication skills and participated in an organized program. They outlined five characteristics:

> Understanding, acceptance, caring, commitment and genuineness are terms that are easily understood and can provide a peer facilitator with a basic understanding of the helping relationship. Moreover, the characteristics of being a good listener and using appropriate interpersonal communication skills appear to complete the picture of an effective peer facilitator.

## Four Important Characteristics

Even though you will be working with younger students, you can help them be more effective facilitators and friendly helpers as they explore the nature of helping relationships. Remembering to keep matters simple, there are four characteristics that might be given special attention: 1) *Caring*; 2) *Accepting;* 3) *Understanding*; and 4) *Trustworthy.* You might include other words or phrases. But, these four can provide meaning without cluttering the training program. They were selected from among all the others because they are relatively easy to comprehend and can make sense to young students. (See *Becoming a Friendly Helper,* Chapter I, pp. 17-18).

Chapter IV in this book describes how these characteristics can be taught to students. However, for your information, these terms are shown with a trainer's definition in Table 3.3.

### Table 3.3

---

**Four Characteristics of a Helping Relationship**

**Caring**—to show a liking or regard, enough to feel concerned or interested and give personal attention.

**Accepting**—to willingly receive and acknowledge the personal worth and dignity of a person, enough to go beyond circumstances.

**Understanding**—to perceive the feeling and meaning of what is said and done, enough to have empathy and a mutual awareness of what is communicated.

**Being Trustworthy**—to be entrusted with confidence, enough to inspire faith, reliance, and a sense of security.

---

**Careful Listening**

Almost every peer counseling or facilitator program that has appeared in the literature emphasized the importance of being an attentive listener. Chapter II in *Becoming a Friendly Helper* also emphasizes the importance of careful listening. All students can improve their listening skills and habits if they: 1) look at the person who is talking; 2) pay attention to the person's words; 3) be aware of the feelings that go with the words; and 4) tell what was heard. These four guidelines were selected and worded accordingly to help young students become better facilitators.

The four guidelines tell the facilitator what to do when listening to someone. They involve eye-contact, being aware of content and feeling, and responding so that people will know that they have been heard.

Some trainers like to encourage their students to be aware of non-verbal behaviors. These may give additional clues as to what a person is thinking and feeling. It's possible that such behaviors may be more powerful in communication than either the spoken or written word. But, interpreting the meaning of non-verbal behaviors requires close study. They can be deceiving and unreliable. Interpreting behavior is risky and not really essential to helping students obtain high levels of communication.

## The Facilitative Responses

The most important part of the helping process is the quality of the relationship. If helpers are to be perceived by helpers as caring, accepting, understanding and trustworthy, what must they do? What are they to say, when they listen to others' concerns and interests? What responses are most helpful and will facilitate others to think about their ideas and feelings?

Samuels and Samuels (1975) reccommended that peer counselors listen carefully, focus on what the "client" is doing physically and how the client feels, not why that person feels a certain way. They further recommended that students not give advice. Besides a few role-playing activities to encourage exploration of some counseling styles, they did not provide a set of facilitative skills.

Gray and Tindall (1978), on the other hand, developed a training program with twelve modules which were designed around some basic communication skills. They recommended a minimum time block of 30 minutes for each module, with 45 to 75 minutes being preferred. In particular, the modules included the skills of attending, empathy (paraphrasing and responding to feelings), summarizing, questioning, genuineness messages ("I" *vs.* "you" statements) and confrontation. Problem-solving procedures were also described.

One of the most impressive features of these modules was a skill-building paradigm with six steps: 1) trainers explain the use and need for skills; 2) trainers model a skill; 3) trainees practice the skill; 4) raters and trainer give feedback to trainees; 5) trainers assign homework and lead discussion of experiences; and 6) trainers and trainees prepare for the next skill. In addition, skill-building modules were arranged in a sequential order and students' skills were evaluated before they participate in some helping roles.

Myrick and Erney (1979) outlined a systematic approach to skill-building for peer facilitators. They began by describing six steps for attentive listening and then presented six response categories that could be used by students to organize their thinking and responding. These were further described as high and low facilitative responses, based upon research and observation (Wittmer and Myrick, 1980).

The six facilitative responses, from lowest to highest, were:

1. Advising and Evaluating
2. Analyzing and Interpreting
3. Reassuring and Supporting
4. Questioning and Probing
5. Clarifying and Summarizing
6. Reflecting and Understanding of Feelings

All of these responses, at one time or another, might be facilitative and no single response by itself can be classified as either good or bad, effective or ineffective. Rather, a response must be considered in light of the situation, time, circumstances, and the probable effect that it might have in a given moment.

This is an important departure from some earlier theorists (e.g. Carkhuff and Berenson, 1967; Gordon, 1970) who tended to rate some responses as categorically facilitative or non-facilitative, helpfulr or nonhelpful, appropriate or inappropriate, and effective or ineffective.

A more detailed discussion of low and high facilitative responses can be found in Wittmer and Myrick (1980) and Myrick and Erney (1978, 1979). But, a brief explanation here can be useful. To begin, the first three categories listed above are viewed as low facilitative and the last three as high facilitative.

**Advising and Evaluating.** Advise and evaluation are considered low facilitative responses because they label or judge people and tell them what to do.

— "You'd better stop picking on Allen, or you're going to get in trouble."

— "You need to talk with your teacher."

— "You should study more."

— "You're just plain lazy."

Such responses tend to make people anxious and defensive. Yet, even though it may be threatening, advice and evaluation can be appropriate when given at the right time. They are generally discouraged as student facilitator responses because most students are already hearing enough of them from teachers, parents, and playmates. As one young boy replied sarcastically when given some "sage" advice, "Oh, yeah... so what else is new?"

**Analyzing and Interpreting.** Analyzing and interpreting responses attempt to tell people what they are thinking and why they are doing what they do.

— "You're just saying that because you don't like me."

— "The reason you don't talk in class is because the kids will laugh at you."

— "You don't like school because you are always getting into trouble."

It is assumed that some hidden causes lurk behind the situation and that if analyzed and interpreted then a problem will be resolved because of the new insights. Unfortunately, it doesn't seem to work that way. Interpretations make most people defensive, and force people to explain themselves. In trying to do so, people often generalize and rationalize instead of revealing an important clue to their behaviors.

Student facilitators do not need to spend time diagnosing, analyzing or interpreting. They are not trained to make diagnoses or prescribe solutions. To the contrary, if they are facilitative, persons being helped will arrive at their own meaningful insights.

**Reassuring and Supporting.** These statements have their place, too, but most people rush in with them, hoping that they are providing some encouragement or building self-confidence. Here are some examples:

— "Everyone feels like that at one time or another."

— "Things could be worse."

— "It may look bad now, but everything is going to turn out alright."

— "Nobody's perfect."

Perhaps only advice is used more often than reassuring and supportive statements by teachers, parents, and would-be helpers. Instead of communicating acceptance and understanding, these responses often tell people that they should not feel as they do and that they should feel something different. While the intent of such statements may be to help a person feel better—and they might do so temporarily—helpees later may think about matters more. Frequently, they feel misunderstood or that their feelings were of little importance to the helper.

These three low facilitative responses are prevelant in daily interactions. You can hear such statements much of the time. Sometimes it takes repeated practice to restrain ourselves from using them and to choose a more high facilitative response; one which is heard less often. Inhibiting or reducing the impulse to rush in with a low facilitative response takes practice.

There is no need to teach students that low facilitative responses are ineffective and should not be used. To the contrary, students should be encouraged to focus on the use of high facilitative responses. In doing so, they automatically reduce the number of low-facilitative responses in their work. Most importantly, as they use more high facilitative responses they become more comfortable with them in their everyday relationships and all aspects of life are improved. Let's take a closer look, now, at the high facilitative responses.

**Open and Closed Questions.** Questions can be either low or high facilitative in nature, depending upon their wording, timing and purpose. Questions can encourage a person to talk and they can keep a discussion going, providing that they are not the only form of response in the discussion. In addition, they keep the attention on the person who is talking. In their own way, they provide some focus or direction to the conversation.

Closed questions usually ask for a "yes" or "no" response and they seldom invite the person to talk more or to elaborate. Open questions, however, require the helpee to share more information. They are often more comforting and inviting. They frequently are perceived as more caring. Look at the following examples:

— "Do you have any brothers or sisters?" (Closed)

— "What can you tell me about your family?" (Open)

— "Do you like school?" (Closed)

— "What do you like about school?" (Open)

*Asking open questions* is one of the three facilitative skills that your students will study in the program. Help them practice using open questions so that they become favored responses rather than ones that occur by chance.

**Clarifying and Summarizing.** Clarifying and summarizing statements are among the highest facilitative responses because they help identify important ideas that are being expressed. They tell people that they are being heard, especially *the events or ideas* that they are describing. Unfortunately, this response is seldom used by parents and teachers (Wittmer and Myrick, 1980) and it may seem a little awkward for students at first.

These responses involve the use of fresh words and they attempt to get to the heart of what is being heard, especially focusing on the events. When used appropriately, helpees will know a helper is listening and have more opportunity to think about what is being said. They can also make corrections if there is some misunderstanding.

— "In other words, you didn't do your homework." (Clarify)

— "Let me see if I'm following you, someone took your books again while you were at lunch." (Clarify)

— "I heard you say two things, you like basketball, but you're not on a team." (Summarize)

— "You told me these things: you're new here; you don't have any friends; but, you do like talking with Judy." (Summarize)

**Reflecting and Understanding of Feelings.** This is perhaps one of the most difficult responses for adults to learn. Young people, however, with training and practice seem to learn the skill quickly. Perhaps they have less social history to contend with and are more open to new ways of expressing themselves. Nevertheless, these responses are considered to be the soul of a helping relationship. They, above all others, communicate a deeper sense of caring, acceptance, and understanding.

— "You're really angry."
— "You're feeling sad."
— "That's very exciting for you."
— "You're happy with your grade."

The very nature of these responses is more intimate. Such responses go beyond the words that are expressed and touch upon what a person is experiencing. Therefore, if not immediately followed by low facilitative responses, they lay the foundation for trust and self-disclosure, all of which lead to more personal awareness and understanding. Without these responses, a helper will always be limited in facilitating others to think about themselves and their actions.

Therefore, student facilitators are encouraged to listen for pleasant and unpleasant feelings and to tell the feelings that they are hearing when they are working with others students (See *Becoming a Friendly Helper*, Chapter III, pp. 35-60). If they are inaccurate, a helpee can always correct them and the communication is clarified. In this process, the relationship becomes closer and there are more opportunities for friendly help.

## Facilitative Feedback

Feedback is telling other people the kind of impact that they are having on you. It is important to understand this concept of feedback because it enables helpers (and helpees) to speak up about behavior and feelings that they experience. Moreover, it also enables the them to communicate the feelings that they are experiencing and what those feelings make them want to do. These thoughts led to the development of a three-step feedback model described by Myrick and Erney (1978) and is called "facilitative feedback."

**Part 1:** *Be specific about the behavior.* What has the person done? Give an example and be descriptive.

**Part 2:** *Tell how the person's behavior makes you feel.* What feelings—pleasant or unpleasant—do you experience when in the presence of the behavior?

**Part 3:** *Tell what your feelings make you want to do.* As a consequence of your feelings, what are you wanting to do?

While the three high facilitative responses cited earlier are powerful tools for student facilitators, you will be handicapped if unable to compliment or confront others. Feedback is an honest reaction to someone.

— "When you said you liked my class project (Step 1; The Behavior), it made me happy (Step 2; The Feeling), and I want to work some more on it (Step 3; The Consequence of the Feeling)."

— "When you showed me around school my first day (Step 1); I was glad (Step 2), and I wanted to thank you (Step 3)."

— "When you said I was stupid and started calling me names (Step 1), I got so mad (Step 2), that I decided not to play with you any more (Step 3)."

— "I feel kinda' down right now (Step 2), and don't want to play anymore (Step 3). You never pass me the ball (Step 1)."

Feedback is such a powerful communication skill that it also needs to be presented to young facilitators in an organized and meaningful way (See *Becoming a Friendly Helper*, Chapter V, pp. 79-90). Therefore, these three steps are re-worded for younger students in the following guidelines:

1. *Be Specific About What You See and Hear.*
2. *Tell What You Are Feeling.*
3. *Tell What Your Feelings Make You Want To Do.*

In addition to the straight forward and direct approach outlined here, it is also possible to communicate thoughts and feelings about someone through an indirect approach (See Myrick and Erney, 1978), which uses metaphors or images:

> "You remind me of a big old bear who just barges in and pushes people around. Sometimes, I just want to run away because it's scary being around big old bears."
>
> "You're a lot like a birthday present. I'm never quite sure what to expect, but you're usually lots of fun."
>
> "When I see you, it makes me remember someone from *Star Wars*. You like to talk about space ships and wierd creatures. Sometimes its fun and other times, you get on my nerves."

Other feedback models and procedures have also been described (e.g. Gray and Tindall, 1978, who focused on confrontation; Gordon, 1970, who described "I" messages).

These also may be helpful in your work. However, the approach outlined here can be used to compliment or confront and has been used successfully by young students.

## Responsible Decision-Making

All of us have goals in life and we try to take steps that help us achieve them. It's easier when you know what you want and when you have the skills to make it happen. Most of us, however, encounter moments along the way when we must make decisions that will either move us toward our goal or set us off on different tangents. In those times, we experience more stress and tension. Sometimes we worry whether or not we have the ability to follow through on our decisions, or whether the decision is the best one we can make. We might worry unnecessarily over the smallest of choices when there is uncertainity in our minds or if we are unsure of our alternatives and consequences.

When problem moments loom up in our lives, decision-making or problem-solving skills play an even more important role. Stress runs higher and there is a tendency to be more confused. Sometimes the pressure of resolving the problem adds to the uncertainty and can lead us to make a hasty and inappropriate decision. In these cases, we might complain about our situation, look for external causes to blame, and be defensive about taking responsibility for our behavior.

On occasion, when a problem seems insurmountable, the situation becomes more distressful and we believe there are few choices. Even these choices sometimes seem beyond our control and we are overwhelmed with "choice-anxiety." What should we do? What if things don't work out right? What if. . . ? Unfortuantely, the "what ifs" often get in the way of making a decision and the "I can'ts" keep us from taking responsibility.

These concepts are important ones for children to learn: 1) everyone has decisions to make and problems to solve; 2) there are ways to help us make decisions and solve problems; and, 3) each of us must accept responsibility for our actions. (See *Becoming a Friendly Helper,* Chapter IV, pp. 61-78).

Gray and Tindall (1978) concentrated their peer training program on problem-solving. They viewed peer counselors as helpers who work with students who had problems and were experiencing trouble, although this is too narrow a focus for most facilitator programs. Their problem-solving module outlined seven steps that students learned to use: exploring the problem, understanding the problem, defining it, brainstorming, evaluating alternatives, deciding the best alternative and implementing it.

In addition, they described some specific communication skills that might best be used with each of the seven stages. The authors felt indebted to the work of Carkhuff and his associates. Their problem-solving model closely approximates that suggested by Carkhuff in his book, *The Art of Problem Solving* (1973).

Myrick and Erney (1978) outlined a five step decision-making process. Recognizing that not all situations allowed for a carefully thought out plan, the five steps were designed to help people explore the decisions (or problems) that face them and to accept responsibility for whatever action is taken— no matter the results. The five steps were: 1) Identify the central issue or problem; 2) Explore the issue or problem; (alternative and consequences); 3) Choose a next step; 4) Act upon your choice; and 5) Evaluate the results.

No doubt, there are other decision-making and problem-solving models available. Young students can be introduced to the fact that everyone has problems sometimes and that, even though no one has discovered a sure way of solving problems, there are five important questions or quidelines that can be useful. The five questions are:

1. *What is the problem?*
2. *What have you tried?*
3. *What else could you do and what would happen if you did that?*
4. *What is your next step?*
5. (later) *How did it go?*

Students can use all of the facilitative responses to explore a problem or decision that is to be made. This five step model is slightly different from others that have been cited in that it focuses upon what has been done, what could be done and a next step. In addition, facilitators can learn the five questions and use them as a guide while they are interviewing someone.
at each step a facilitator is encouraged to ask questions, clarify and summarize statements, and respond to feelings. Thus, the question (or steps) in combination with the facilitative responses provide a simple and convienient structure to us when working with students and adults, either individually or in groups.

This particular model has been used successfully by students as young as third graders to help others make decisions and solve problems. One sixth grade boy, Sam, interviewed a teacher who was having problems with some of her students. The young facilitator taped his after school session with the teacher and it was easy to hear him lead the teacher through the first four steps, while making clarifying and feeling responses. Sam was thrilled to help a teacher explore a problem. The teacher, who volunteered to be in a facilitator project in order to help a student, was surprised at how easy it was to talk with Sam and how much she learned about herself and the classroom situation.

## Assessment of Self and Others

One of the strengths of Gray and Tindall's school peer counseling program is that se[veral] procedures were part of the training module[s...] trainer to evaluate the progress that students [out]comes for different stages are clearly define[d...] evaluation easier. In addition, the evaluatio[n...] used by the trainees themselves, taking the form of narrative comments, observations, and completion of rating sheets.

You will want to know how your students are progressing through the training sessions. You can use several different methods to evaluate the training process. This might be done, for example, through some short written tests in which students choose or write responses to given situations. Or, it might be done through role-playing exercises, in which students put theory into practice and give a response or make a series of responses. Direct observation and timely instruction can be powerful tools. In addition, you may want to have students complete some homework assignments, either written or taped.

Tape recordings of an interaction with someone can help you identify strengths in the helping process and areas that need improvement. You may also want to rely on the observations of others (e.g. teachers, students or parents).

Checklists can be used to assist people in their evaluations. For example, two facilitators can be paired to work with a student. One initiates the discussion and leads the way, while the other takes notes—especially on the responses and work of the other facilitator. Feedback can be given later.

Sometimes these assessments in the training program will also help students to learn more about themselves, as well as the helping process. This experience of self-exploration and self-discovery is one of the most stimulating and rewarding aspects of being a student facilitator. While facilitators like to help others and take part in projects, most enjoy learning more about themselves and the reactions of others to them.

assessment can focus on the helping skills, but it also becomes an important educational experiencae when attention is given to other aspects, such as physical self, personal beliefs and attitudes, general skills and abilities, and relationships with others. Self-understanding and understanding others go hand-in-hand in setting realistic goals and having self-confidence in accomplishing them. (See *Becoming a Friendly Helper*, Chapter VI, pp. 91-110).

In summary, it is recommended that your program center around the following basic concepts and skills: 1) the importance and the characteristics of a helping relationship; 2) the three high facilitative responses (open questions, clarifying and summarizing, and responding to feelings); 3) facilitative feedback — complimenting and confronting; 4) five steps to decision-making and problem-solving, and 5) assessing self and others.

There are more ideas that could be included. You may want to add some other concepts and skills. Perhaps you have some favorite expressions that conceptualize helping skills or maybe some important ideas that you want your students to learn. There is nothing wrong with making changes or modifications that suit your interests and needs. Or, you may want to add special components that are particularly suited for your school or community, your students and the projects that you plan for them. However, the ideas presented in this book and *Becoming a Friendly Helper* have been tried and tested. They have been clarified and refined, based upon student input and trainer reactions. You will find them helpful in your work and they can provide a solid foundation upon which to build your program.

## Program Trainer or Coordinator

Perhaps the most important question for any student facilitator program is: Who will be the trainer or coordinator? The answer often depends upon the extent of the program and the kind of projects that are implemented. Yet, there are a few other factors that should be considered.

Above all else, the coordinator or trainer is usually someone who is interested and enthusiastic about the idea of children helping children through an organized and systematic student facilitator program. If you are to be this person, you might ask yourself these questions: How much time am I willing to give the program, in addition to my other duties and responsibilities? Is this program and its concepts something that captures my imagination and stimulates my creativity? Am I committed enough to follow through with all parts of the program— selection of students, training, projects, supervising and evaluating?

Observation suggests that personal characteristics of the trainer are probably more important than prior knowledge or experience with program concepts and projects. This book, and others, can provide some guidelines and activities which will assist you. It can be helpful if you are already familiar with the concepts that have been outlined above. If not, there are several references and resources that will help you bridge the gap.

School counselors are often identified as the most likely persons in elementary and middle schools to start and coordinate student facilitator programs. In general they have received more graduate preparation in human behavior and interpersonal relationships. Yet, most admit that they, too, need some additional study before they feel comfortable developing a comprehensive student facilitator program.

Teachers can also be coordinators. Some have preferred to be co-directors or co-coordinators because of their classroom commitments. Their time is not often flexible. If they initiate a program within the context of a class, which is possible, they might work with larger numbers of students and make adjustments accordingly. One teacher was so determined to start a program that she volunteered to meet students after school until training was completed. Then, during lunch time, she planned projects with the students.

It is also possible to provide an intensive one-day workshop for student facilitators, where most of the concepts and skills are introduced. This enables teachers, as well as counselors and others, to continue with their regular schedules.

Principals and support personnel can also serve as coordinators. Again, flexibility of time may enable them to be candidates for the coordinator or trainer's role, providing that they also have the commitment and enthusiasm. A principal might, for example, incorporate all or part of the training program in student council meetings or with a school patrol group.

It should be remembered, at this point, that there are different kinds of training programs and that student facilitators, depending upon their training, can become involved in limited or extensive projects. Some schools begin student facilitator programs on a small basis and attempt to move them toward more comprehensive ones, where students can be actively involved in all of the helping roles described in this book.

Will you be the coordinator? If not, who will you recommend? What support will you need, or be able to give? What steps are needed to help you get organized?

# Chapter IV
# Getting Organized

There are many people who like the idea of children helping children. It's easy to get enthusiastic about the potential of a program that systematically prepares children for some helping roles. But, it takes something extra to go beyond the initial stage of interest.

Making a commitment is probably the first and most important step toward developing a student facilitator program. Then, you can concentrate your energies on getting organized and taking some next steps in building a program. These include developing or forming an over-all plan from which to work, seeking and obtaining some support, and involving students through a fair and suitable selection process. This chapter will focus upon these next steps.

| Step 1: Making A Commitment |
| --- |
| **Step 2: Forming a Plan** |

Can you imagine building a house without a plan? There was a man who decided to build on an addition to his house. He collected a lot of materials and one day when he was feeling energetic he launched into the project, as if it would be completed before nightfall. Before long, it became obvious that he did not have a suitable plan. He had some interesting ideas—a fireplace, a double-wide door onto a deck, and some benches here and there—but no specific plan to follow.

Consequently, he made many adjustments as he moved along. Sometimes things worked out well and, just as often, sometimes they didn't. It was a piecemeal project, one born of enthusiasm and excitement, but ill-planned. Before long, some of the problems became tedious. There was a lot of un-doing, re-doing, and starting over again. His energy was wasted frequently, even though he didn't seem to mind. When he made a mistake, he would exclaim, "Well, I'm learning this time, but next time, I'll...." Even before the project was finished, he was already talking about "next time."

Learning the hard way—through experience—has its value. It can be intrinsically rewarding. Most of us have taken part in projects that required courage because we didn't have the experience, know-how, or skill. Sometimes these projects worked out and sometimes they didn't.

Almost everyone would agree that a general plan can help avoid some pitfalls and can save time in the long run. A plan can give you direction, provide some guidelines from which to deviate, if you choose, and help you chart a course of action. In this sense, forming a plan for a student facilitator program can be useful.

It may not be possible in this chapter to outline all of the components that you will want in your initial plan. Yet, there are a few basics that you will want to include. They give a clearer idea of your commitment.

## Who Will Be Trained as Facilitators?

As you begin to think about building a program, it is natural to turn your attention to students that you would enjoy working with again. Or, you might be thinking about a particular group of students who would especially benefit from the experience, as well as provide some valuable assistance to others.

Will you work with high-performing students? Or, will you include others? What kind of personal characteristics will be a part of the selection criteria? What grade or age levels will be sources of helpers and helpees? Do you have a particular project in mind that requires a certain kind of student? These and other selection factors must be considered in forming a plan. Some of the answers may be influenced by the number of facilitators you plan to train at one time and subsequent projects.

One practical approach is to select those who are already identified as "stars" or "natural leaders" in the school. These are usually older students who have performed well in their classrooms and who are also popular with their classmates. These same students often display a kind of energetic personality. They seem to have the extra time and interest to work on special projects outside the classroom, while keeping up with their academic studies. You may want to begin your program with this kind of student. There are some advantages.

Teachers frequently look for extra activities for these students because they tend to finish their class work early. Some teachers believe that these students have the ability to be facilitators in cross-age level projects and the experience adds to their academic gains. Teachers also tend to give them more responsibility and freedom to move about. They enjoy the trust and respect of the faculty. In addition, these students are quick learners, eager to get involved, and reliable. They have a way of making teachers and counselors feel successful.

On occasion, a student facilitator program is viewed as a "leadership class" for those who have leadership potential. In some instances, the program has appealed to teachers who are responsible for working with "gifted" students, especially those who lack social skills. A case for using high-performing students in projects is usually easier to build than one for low-performing students.

Low-performing students can benefit from being student facilitators too. Sometimes the experience is just the right "treatment" for a child who lacks self-confidence and who needs a boost in self-esteem.

Giving a low-performing student some responsibility can sometimes spark that student to become more responsible and motivated. The program could provide the information, experiences, and rewards that enable low-performing students to achieve more. It gives them recognition and helps them to feel more important and needed. It's a self-concept builder and provides a launching pad for a new way of learning for some students.

In thise sense, "training is treatment" and perhaps more acceptable to students than confrontation, teacher encouragement, or even personal counseling. However, to begin a program with a majority of low-performing students is risky and you may want to include only a few at first.

These "target children" take extra time and need closer supervision, as a general rule. Moreover, a training group composed predominantly of children who are in need of special help can limit the program's contribution to a school, although it certainly is a viable approach to working with students who have adjustment problems.

Some of the more desirable characteristics of students selected to be facilitators have typically included the following:

1. Verbal Ability—Can they express their ideas well and in an organized manner?

2. Intellectual Ability—Can they grasp ideas quickly so that they can be trained in a relatively short period of time?

3. Leadership Potential—Do other students respect and listen to them?

4. Age-Grade Level—Can they work with same-age or younger students?

5. Motivation—Are they enthusiastic about joining the program?

6. Responsibility—Can they initiate and complete projects on their own with minimal supervision?
7. Attitude Toward Others—Do they have a positive view of others and a genuine desire to help?

Some program coordinators may prefer to work only with student volunteers, perhaps having a sign-up list and then narrowing the selection based upon other considerations. The assumption is that volunteers will have more interest and commitment than ones who have no choice (e.g. a small group of students drawn at random from a class, or a class of fifth graders whose teacher believed that facilitator training was appropriate for the entire class). In general, when students have no choice in participating, training outcomes are more limited and projects are more specifically focused (e.g. each sixth grade student, upon completion of training, might be assigned a second grade student to tutor for five sessions in a five week project).

In some instances, the coordinator may seek out and encourage a student to become a facilitator. For example, one counselor wanted to insure that three young girls whom he had been helping would join the program. These students lacked self-confidence and motivation. When school work became more difficult, they had a tendency to quit easily. They rarely volunteered for anything in class. Before announcing the program to the school, the counselor met with the girls in his office and described what he felt was a special opportunity for them.

"You know, you are really special in many ways and we need your help. There are some younger students in our school that we'd like you to work with, but first there is a training program that will prepare you to be a 'friendly helper' and get you ready to work with them. We would especially like you to sign up for the program when it is announced this week." The girls smiled and looked at each other shyly as they heard the counselor talk about them. The program provided an opportunity to get them more involved in school and to learn more about themselves in the process.

For some coordinators, the primary consideration in selecting students is whether they are accesible and available for projects. It is assumed that the training sessions are an important part of the school curriculum and that students could be chosen at random. Some students may not progress through the training as fast as others or become as adept at facilitating. Consequently, they may not be able to work in all of the roles outlined in this book.

Some procedures for selecting students will be described later in this chapter. But, it is worthy of note at this point that your own personal preferences, limitations, and expectations will play an important role in final selection of students. As you become more experienced as a program coordinator, you will probably expand your selections.

## How Many Facilitators Should be Trained?

Ideally, all students should be trained to be "facilitators." Can you imagine how this would affect the learning climate? It would reduce the number of crises and conflicts that are now a typical part of most school days. Students would have the skills to help resolve difficulties. Learning and personal relationships would be improved.

This might be accomplished by adapting the program to the classroom curriculum and working with an entire class. Large group instruction is possible. However, while many may learn the skills, it's difficult to devise and supervise helping projects for so many students at one time. In addition, not all students progress at the same pace and training is less manageable with a large group. While it can be done, it is an ambitious task and there is usually something lost in the process, especially when attempted at first.

A large number of students might be reached by rotating small groups of students through the training sessions. But, expediency and teaching all students are not the most important considerations for a student facilitator program.

It is also possible to train an individual student. Although a one-to-one situation may have some benefits in terms of personal attention, it lacks the benefit of group dynamics and limits training. For instance, the student would not have peers to offer support, feedback and reactions to ideas.

Most students are trained in small groups outside the classroom, perhaps 6-10 students per group. When training is presented in smaller groups, there is more active participation, more individual attention, more follow-up, and projects are more manageable. The number of small groups to be trained in the course of one year will depend upon trainer interests and schedule limitations. Typically, the coordinator will work closely with about 10-12 student facilitators per year and these students will be more actively involved in projects than others who might just experience some of the training.

## How Will You Train Them?

Some school counselors who attended a national guidance conference asked, "What is the training program like?" They wanted to know the kind of activities young students could experience that would make them facilitators. The answer, of course, was more complex than simply identifying some fun activities.

First, you will want to know something about the students who will be taking part in your training sessions. However, for the most part, it can be assumed that regardless of age or ability all will need some skill training in the communication and the helping relationship. No single activity or set of activities can guarantee results. Yet, with careful planning and with some sequential experiences, students can be led to be facilitators in the roles of assistants, tutors, special friends and small group leaders.

The training sessions outlined in Chapter V provide a basic structure from which you can work. The sessions were designed so that students could move progressively toward the goal of being a "friendly helper." But, it is possible to design your own program around other activities and experiences, perhaps some that appeal to you more than those described. The important point is to have a rationale upon which to build a program and not be caught in the trap of leading children through some "fun and games," hoping that they can learn to facilitate others.

The other part of the answer to the question rests in your plans for the facilitators after they have completed training. Chapter VI contains some ideas regarding projects—beginning, intermediate and advanced. As you pick projects for students, analyze the skills that are required. Preparation is the key to developing a popular and successful student facilitator program.

You will also want to consider the students who will be the helpees—the ones receiving help from the facilitators. What assumptions, if any, might be made about them as a project begins? What fundamental procedures need to be included in training, besides the focus upon interpersonal communication? Chapter V is a starting place. How much training is needed will depend upon your students, their progress, goals, and projects.

## Training Sessions: Where and When?

Training sessions can occur in a number of places. Preferably, you will want a quiet place where the facilitators can practice their skills without interruption and where discussion can be heard. For a small group (6-8), training might take place in the guidance office or the counselor's room. Some trainers have worked with students in hallways, the back of cafeterias, outside and under some shade trees, media centers, and makeshift closets. Ideally, there should be enough room for experiential activities and, in almost every case, the seating arrangement is a circular one. Tables are optional and usually viewed as barriers—to be removed so that the students can work more closely with one another and establish better eye contact.

When will you meet with the facilitators for training and supervision? The answer is related to the logistics of the program, your time commitments and the use of space. Facilitators could attend the training sessions during a specified time rather than remain in their classroom. Specific times for training should be arranged by "contracting" between you and the classroom teacher. Teachers are much more likely to cooperate when they know when and how long students will be gone.

They don't want to be surprised or put in a position of having to repeat instructions or tests. Contracts, either written or informally agreed upon, remind the teacher of the released time for your program. In the event that a student is absent from a classroom activity or test, the contract assures the student of not being penalized.

## How Many Sessions?

The number of sessions, of course, will depend upon your objectives and whether or not you have a beginning or advanced program. Advanced projects take more training and preparation. Most coordinators meet their facilitators for about 30-40 minutes per training session. The sessions in Chapter V are based upon this time allotment, but adjustments can be made.

"Marathon training" might be appropriate for some schools, especially where teachers are reluctant to release students for training sessions over several weeks. In a marathon, more sessions are offered in an extended time period (e.g. four sessions in one morning, where students remain with a trainer for about 2 1/2 hours, including appropriate rest periods.)

While such an approach has the advantages of concentrated effort, continutity, efficient use of time, and assured attendance, it also has the disadvantage of eliminating homework, some practice time, and the opportunity for moving students at a learning pace that suits them best. Marathon training can be fatiguing and some excitement can be lost as quickly as it it gained.

In Gainesville, Florida, three middle school counselors and their colleagues agreed to work together in a day-long training session for their student facilitators. During the first year each counselor selected 12 students to bring to the "Student Facilitator Workshop" which was held in a large clubhouse located in a residential area. The 36 students met together from 8:30 a.m. until 4:30 p.m. on Friday, a teacher workday. A series of training activities focused on helping relationship concepts and the facilitative responses. Brown-bag lunches, with snacks at break-times, added to the group's cohesiveness and unique learning experiences. Friendships between schools were formed and positive testimonies emphasized how much students and counselors enjoyed the day.

Later, at their respective schools, the facilitators continued to meet with their counselors for more training and to think about projects where they might use their new skills. One counselor met daily with her facilitators during luchtime until a schedule of projects was arranged. The next year, approximately 100 students participated in the workshop from five schools. This required additional personnel to assist the trainers. Small group participation was still the favored mode of training, although there were some large group presentations.

## When Will You Start?

The best time to start is when you feel prepared and have the kind of support that you think is necessary. You may want to try a "pilot program" with a few students (perhaps two or three, although the training sessions in Chapter V are designed for six). You can adapt the program to one or two students.

If this is the first time that a program has been implemented in your school, teachers may want you to wait a few weeks after the beginning of school.year. This gives them a chance to know their students, establish a routine, and make lesson plans accordingly. An ideal time to start a first year program is in the middle of the school year, Usually in January. As one counselor observed, there are too many adjustments to be made in early fall and too many national holidays in late fall and December which interrupt training.

If the program is continuing from the preceeding year, experienced student facilitators might begin some fall projects. Most trainers agree that even experienced facilitators need some additional training and supervision, although probably not as intense as it was in the beginning. Coordinating your training program with a group of teachers and finding the right combination of students takes time and effort, but the more attention you give to these matters, the fewer conflicts and cancellations you will experience later on.

You may not have all the answers for a complete plan, but you should have an over-all picture of your program and what it is about. It can be helpful if you take a calendar and plot a schedule of events and important timelines. It might show some deadlines, starting and ending points, and some projects and activities. This will be valuable as you think about what you will tell others and how you can enlist their support.

> Step 1: Making a Commitment
> Step 2: Forming a Plan
>
> **Step 3: Enlisting Support**

To develop a comprehensive program, you will need support from several groups. Faculty, administration, students, and parents are important support groups that are needed from the beginning. It is probably unrealistic to worry about and seek unanimous support and understanding from everyone in a school and community. Yet, some alliances are necessary to the survival and success of a program. Timely support can keep you from feeling isolated and provide some valuable sources for suggestions and feedback. Those who believe in your ideas can help you with those who may be initially skeptical of new and different approaches, regardless of proven effectiveness or good intentions.

**Interested Teachers**

You can start by identifying some initially supportive teachers. Think about those with whom you feel most comfortable and enjoy sharing ideas. Some may have already expressed interest in a program. Others may be those who like to try new things and keep up with contemporary ideas in education. Still others may come to mind because they feel secure with administrators and parents. Or, you might begin with those who would be most receptive to particular helping projects. Regardless of who and how many teachers you include in this initial support group, talk with them about your general plan and strategies. Get some initial feedback. They can help you identify what's missing in your plan, the obstacles, some priorities and assets.

The following ideas may be helpful:

— Talk with the person in the school with whom you feel closest. Share your ideas.

— Identify some small group interraction. Seek out their reactions.

— Ask a small group of teachers to meet with you over lunch to explore the basic idea and some of your plans.

— Give these same teachers an article or book on the subject to read before or after the meeting. Make copies of a brief excerpt, remembering how busy teachers are with their own work.

— Have a group of teachers help you identify some important needs in the school that would be amenable to a student facilitator program.

— Ask some teachers to identify a few students who would especially benefit from a peer helper.

— Encourage teachers to help you identify some projects that would help meet student needs and fit into the school's schedule.

**Administration**

Administrators ultimately set the climate of the school. If your school has an approachable principal with whom you have a close working relationship, then you will want to talk with that person about your ideas, as soon as possible. If there is distance or if you are unsure of the principal's reaction, you can "test the waters" through some selected teachers who might help you think of ways to present your plan.

Administrators should not be taken for granted. They want to know what's happening in their schools. Although they are busy and may not take time to hear about every detail, nevertheless they want to be informed about your intentions. Here are some things you might do:

— Meet with a friend and try out your presentation to the principal, encouraging your friend to force you to examine the pros and cons.

— Pick a time when the administrator is most likely to have time to hear your plan and discuss it with you. Avoid stressful times.

— Be prepared to leave an outline or some key ideas in writing. Make a note of your meeting and any supportive remarks so that you can refer to them later.

— Loan a copy of this book to administrators. Smile when they tell you that they read this recommendation.

— Invite the adminstrator to sit in on a planning session with two or three of your supportive teachers.

— Identify some other schools in your area who may be implementing a similar program and, with the principal, go there for a visit.

— Be aware of how the program can benefit students as facilitators, students as helpees and the faculty. Show how these benefits are related to your needs assessment.

— Be prepared to use facilitative skills in exploring ideas, and use feedback responses.

— Be positive and avoid being defensive.

You may need to make some adaptations, perhaps incorating your program into already existing school programs. For example, one school prepared safety patrol members to be better leaders and friendly helpers through facilitator training. In another school, a teacher had facilitator training as a unit in social studies. You may need to start small and build toward a more comprehensive program. Your administrator can help you identify some progressive stages.

## Faculty

At this point, you may be ready to talk with all the faculty as a group. You need their support, but not all of the faculty need to be directly involved. Still, they all want to be informed. A faculty meeting will alert them to what you're doing. Keep your presentation short and to the point. Or, you may prefer to meet with the faculty in smaller groups, perhaps by grade levels. You might:

— Begin by asking if they could use some more help in their classes with some particular students. Then, talk about how these students might benefit from working with other students.

— Show the group a film about peer facilitators (e.g. *Peer Facilitators: Youth Helping Youth; Developmental Counseling in the Elementary School*).

— Obtain a slide program from a program coordinator in another school.

— Invite another program coordinator to help you present the idea and share experiences.

— Make a video tape of some students in action and use it to make a case for a more organized and systematic training program with special projects.

**Students**

Student enthusiasm can be a powerful motivator for adults. A presentation might be made to students in an assembly or in classrooms. If you already have trained some facilitators they might help you. Or, they might do it themselves. In addition, you could:

— Talk enthusiastically with the students about the selection process. It can make a critical difference in student perceptions and support.

— Depending upon the age of the students, prepare a brief description of your plans, including training and possible projects.

— Make announcements through classroom presentations, school newspapers, bulletin boards, or over the intercom.

— Put some students on your planning committee.

— Prepare a demonstration activity for students and faculty.

— After facilitators have been trained and projects have been identified, prepare the other students for their services and help through appropriate presentations and announcements.

— Use student testimonials as support and encouragement.

**Parents**

The student facilitator program must be seen as a part of the school's academic and guidance program. Parental permission for participation is, therefore, assumed. In cases where written permission has been required, programs have tended to be more limited and there is often more misunderstanding. Written permission is sometimes percieved as a method of releasing the school of responsibility for something which involves a high risk. Some parents, not understanding the program, may not give permission, thus limiting opportunities for many needy and deserving students.

Just as parents are informed of other interesting and beneficial projects at the school, you might send a letter home about the program and its potential. They like hearing about accomplishments. The P.T.A. might also be a place to inform parents. Some parents could volunteer to assist you on some selected projects, thus becoming more positively involved in the school. When appropriate, you may even want to take a few parents through some of the same communication exercises that students experienced.

Support is something that will grow as your program progresses. Success tends to breed more success and attract attention. This is going to be the case in the development of your student facilitator program.

> Step 1: Making a Commitment
> Step 2: Forming a Plan
> Step 3: Enlisting Support
>
> **Step 4: Selecting Student Facilitators**

In schools where student facilitator programs exist, there are numerous students who want to take part. Some want to be facilitators because they once received help. Others hear about the personal attention given in training and the opportunities to learn more about self and others. A few want the recognition. How will you select your students? Who will be the student facilitators?

**The Invitation**

First, you will want to decide the grade level or age group that will participate. Some coordinators have worked with cross-age groups, drawing from different classrooms. It was their intent to have at least two facilitators at each grade level.

In general, it seems best to have about six students in a training group who are at the same age level . This offers advantages when projects are designed and implemented with younger students. In addition, the students can co-lead groups or be group facilitators for their classrooms (See Chapter VI).

There are several ways to extend an invitation. If it is going to be a small select group and one that you have identified, then there may be no need for elaborate selection procedures. You simply meet with those students you've identified, tell them about the program and its potential, listen to their reactions, and obtain a commitment if they are interested. This can be done quietly or with fan-fare, depending upon your own interests and the need to motivate the students.

On the other hand, you can increase interest and motivation in the student body through publicized selection procedures. For example, after appropriate announcements have been made in some classes, sign-up lists might be used for interested students. Or, a more formal application might be available, and students could complete it (See Figure 4.1).

**Figure 4.1: An Invitation**

Student Facilitator Group
Spring Hill Middle School

Student Facilitators work with other students. They are guidance assistants. They are trained by the school counselor to be effective listeners. In addition, they are given systematic training in interpersonal skills, which they use to help others talk about their ideas and feelings. They work through carefully organized and supervised guidance activities. As they help others learn, they learn about themselves. Interested?

A Facilitator is a person who:

1. is easy to get along with and who is capable of helping others.
2. has the personal traits of: acceptance, patience, a sense of humor, and caring about others.
3. has positive attitudes towards peers, school, and adults.

Responsibilities and helping projects may include:

1. Serve as peer tutors.
2. Assist teachers.
3. Help orient new students.
4. Lead small group discussions.
5. Provide role models.
6. Host visitors to the school.
7. Plan and conduct the fourth grade orientation program to the middle school.
8. Assist the counselor.
9. Be available to students who need "someone to talk with."
10. Represent and/or make presentations to interested groups such as service clubs and Parent Advisory Council.

Still interested?

If interested, fill out an application form. Final selections will be based on teacher recommendations and counselor selection.

Extending an invitation might be done in several ways:
— Announce your program over the intercom. Interested students might attend a meeting during the afternoon recess or break period. At this meeting, you can make a presentation and provide a sign-up list.
— Make arrangements with the teachers to visit classes for 15 minute presentations about the program. Interested students might write one page about, "Why I Would Like To Be A Friendly Helper."
— Ask interested students to fill out a self-evaluation. Teachers might also complete one for the students.
— Meet with some teachers after school and, together, compile a list of students who might benefit and be considered.
— Ask interested students to sign-up for a brief interview. During the interview, look for desired characteristics in the students. Immediately following each interview, a criteria check-list can be filled out for each student.

A middle school counselor started a program with a group of eighth grade students (about 10). Students volunteered for the program or were recommended by teachers. In addition, they were students that she knew and whom she thought might be effective facilitators. In the second year of the program she decided to offer an open invitation to students across grade levels (6-8). Announcements (See Figure 4.1) were posted outside the guidance office, on student bulletin boards, and in the general teaching areas. Approximately 75 students applied. It made the selection process more challenging and difficult, but students who were finally selected were excited and loyal to the program.

## Making the Selections

After you have received the applications, review them and narrow the list. Some coordinators and trainers prefer to meet individually with each applicant, using the opportunity to give the students some personal attention and learn more about them. Others prefer to make their selections and then meet individually with those who were not selected, giving them an opportunity to talk about their feelings and what they might do as an alternative. However, when an invitation is issued to a large population and a large group applies, individual interviews for either screening or follow-up may not be as practical.

Sometimes students can be screened in groups, perhaps using a guidance activity that involves self-disclosure and requires sensitive listening. This might help identify those students who already have an inclination toward being careful listeners and responsive to the interests and needs of others. On the other hand, the training sessions will help those who are less skillful in the beginning. A lack of skill should not be a determining factor.

You will, no doubt, have your own screening criteria. A checklist might be devised. One coordinator used experienced student facilitators to help interview applicants and received confidential ratings from each one. Final selection remained with the trainer and coordinator.

There are different ways in which students can be informed about your selections. Again, this may depend upon the publicity given the program and the number who applied. A small number of applicants probably means that you can meet with all students, either individually or in small groups, to tell them about the results. This is especially critical if your program is limited in the number of students that will be trained.

For example, if you decide to work with only 10-15 students for the school year, then your selections will be received with even more acclaim. If you plan to begin with one group and start another upon completion of the first group's training, there is more hope for those who may not have been selected in the first round.

One coordinator selected twenty students at the beginning of the school year to take part in training sessions and subsequent projects. Because of the large number of applicants, the couselor decided to send each one a memo rather that risk that students would learn of their selection or rejection from a second-hand source. These brief letters are seen in Figures 4.2 and 4.3.

**Figure 4.2**

**An Acceptance Letter**

---

January 4

Dear _____

Congratulations! It is my pleasure to inform you that you have been selected to be a student facilitator. It is going to be an exciting time and I hope one of the most rewarding experiences you'll ever have.

Please meet with us Friday, January 7, at (time) in the guidance office. Come prepared to get involved in the challenging opportunity of helping others.

Sincerely yours,

Dot Thomas, Coordinator
Student Facilitator Program
Spring Hill Middle School

---

Children Helping Children

**Figure 4.3**

**An Alternate's Letter**

---

Dear _____

It is very difficult for me to report that you will not be participating in the student facilitator program this year. There were many applications and only a small number could be in the program. A number of things determined the final decisions. Almost everyone who was interviewed would have done well in the program, but it was impossible to work with so large a number.

You have been chosen as an alternate. In the event that more students are needed, you will be considered again. However, there will be some other activities during the year in which you can be a helper. We do need your help.

If you want to discuss this matter, please see me in the guidance office. Thank you for applying!

Sincerely yours,

Dot Thomas, Coordinator
Student Facilitator Program
Spring Hill Middle School

## Obtaining a Commitment

When you first meet with students who have been selected, you can be more specific about your plans and they can help you think through some of the ideas that you have for them. It is important to clarify goals and outline your expectations, which usually includes a brief explanation of the number of training sessions, when you will meet and the duration of each session. You might also want to clarify the kind of roles and projects that might be undertaken later. However, projects can be tailored to the group and too much emphasis upon what is expected of them may make a few unnecessarily worried.

Assure them that they will be receiving the needed training to work in the roles and projects. If students are still interested, then more specific steps can be taken toward the training sessions. If someone cannot make a commitment or has a schedule conflict with the program after hearing your explanations, then it may be necessary to select another student and move along.

One trainer developed an agreement, a "contract," which selected students read, studied for one or two days, and then returned signed by themselves, a witness (another student) and an adult (teacher or parent). Although not a legal document, it added excitement to the program and the young students enjoyed the importance of the procedure.

Another variation is to have a contract between facilitator, classroom teachers and the counselor (See Figure 4.4). This is a clear declaration that a student will be involved and serves the purpose of obtaining written support from faculty who would be affected directly on occasion.

Teachers, for the most part, are very cooperative with the projects, especially when they see how they are relevant to educational objectives. However, teachers have their own plans and don't always appreciate interruptions. For example, one teacher remarked, "I like the counselor and the peer program, however, one of the things I don't like is that our counselor pulls kids out of my class without warning and expects me to cooperate in a minute's notice. I don't want to be difficult, but I have my lesson plans, too, and need to plan accordingly."

With the help of a "contract" there is a mutual agreement as to the times and conditions of the training sessions and projects. No student will be penalized inadvertantly for being a facilitator.

Finally, you may want to take your list of selected students to the principal and classroom teachers to verify any recommendations, qualifications, and faculty commitments for students to be in the program. It's time then to consult your calendar of events and plan for the first training session.

**Figure 4.4**

**A Student Facilitator Contract**

_____ has been selected to participate in the student facilitator program. Training sessions to become a Friendly Helper will begin shortly and upon completion of training, helping projects around the school will take place. It is understood that Friendly Helpers:

1. Attend school regularly
2. Complete class assignments
3. Serve as model students
4. Assist other students
5. Follow school rules

I, _____ hereby agree to conduct myself as a Friendly Helper and to take an active part in the student facilitator program.

_____
Recommendation

_____
Student Signature

_____
Trainer or
Coordinator Signature

# Chapter V
# Training Student Facilitators

> Step 1: Making a Commitment
> Step 2: Forming a Plan
> Step 3: Enlisting Support
> Step 4: Selecting the Facilitators
> **Step 5: Training the Facilitators**

One of the most challenging and rewarding aspects of building a student facilitator program is the development of appropriate training sessions. Training sessions determine the roles and functions that your students can perform. These are, inturn, directly related to the kinds of projects in which the facilitators will take part and the success that they will achieve.

How much training will your students need? The answer depends upon what you want them to do. What roles do you want them to assume? What tasks are to be performed? What degree of success do you want them to obtain? The more you expect of the student facilitators, the more you will want to develop a systematic approach to the training process. Success occurs when careful preparation meets opportunity.

With a systematic approach, concepts and skills are organized into a schematic pattern that is meaningful to young people. There is a set of activities and experiences which sequentially leads trainees toward program objectives. These successive steps give them the skills and self-confidence to provide positive experiences for others and to profit from being a friendly helper.

Sometimes it is difficult to know where to start. There is so much that can be done and so many exciting possibilities. If you are as enthusiastic as most other people who are involved with facilitator programs, you will have to resist the urge to hurry things along. Most of us want to rush into activities and projects that are appealing and immediately useful. If you are impatient, your program may meet with more limited successes. On the other hand, if you are too cautious, the program can begin to "drag" and the enthusiasm and enjoyment of you and your students may decline.

This chapter outlines a series of training sessions that will help prepare your trainees for several different kinds of roles and related projects. The concepts and skills that have been selected represent a basic foundation upon which to build any peer or leadership program. Although adaptations or modifications are possible, the following training sessions will enable your students to work effectively in such roles as student assistants, tutors, special friends, and small group leaders.

In addition, the sessions are arranged in such a way that after some initial training the students can participate in beginning projects. Then, after more training, they can take part in more extended projects. It is the training and the projects themselves that characterize most programs as either beginning, intermediate or advanced.

## How This Chapter is Organized

The remainder of this chapter gives attention to twenty training sessions for student facilitators. Included is an outline for an orientation meeting to help get students started and ready for training. The "beginning program" with related projects is built upon the first ten sessions. Of these, sessions one through nine focus upon the helping relationship and some basic skills for "friendly helpers." In the tenth session, plans are made for their first projects. These ten sessions are organized around the material in the first three chapters of *Becoming a Friendly Helper*.

Sessions 11-15 develop skills needed in an intermediate program with related projects. More specifically, problem-solving and facilitative feedback are learned ( *BFH,* Chapters IV and V). Thereafter, sessions 16-20 complete the training and prepare students for advanced projects (*BFH*, Chapters VI and VII). The completion of all twenty training sessions, with supplementary meetings related to projects and skill development, provide the foundation for a comprehensive student facilitator program.

## The Training Sessions

**Length of Training Sessions.** The training sessions are based upon meetings of approximately 30-45 minutes each. Abilities and interests will influence the speed at which students progress and any adaptations that must be made. If students need more practice with a particular skill, then additional sessions may be added where appropriate. The supplemental activities described in this book can be drawn upon for more practice sessions.

**Reading Assignments.** The length of a session can also be influenced by reading assignments in *Becoming a Friendly Helper*. If students complete the assignments as "homework," more time can be used for activities and discussions in a training session. Training sessions were not designed as reading circles. In some cases, however, the first ten or fifteen minutes of a session might have to be used for reading the assigned lessons. Time has to be adjusted accordingly.

**Duration of Training.** The duration of training may vary too, depending upon the schedule established by a trainer and the trainee groups. The sessions might be arranged over several weeks, perhaps once a week for twenty weeks. But, this is not the preferred approach. If too much time passes between sessions, continuity is lost.

Many trainers prefer meeting their groups twice a week until students are ready for projects. Thereafter, the groups meet once a week, at the same time, or at a more convenient time (e.g. lunch, before or after school, activity period, recess, or Saturday mornings).

In addition, supplementary activities can extend training, especially if more practice in some skills is needed prior to a project. Otherwise, these extra activities can be used for review later or as part of supervision. Finally, additional meetings may be needed for specific preparation of certain tasks, activities, procedures, or logistics associated with a special project.

Ideally, the twenty training sessions might be achieved within 10-12 weeks. For example, one trainer met with two groups of trainees on Tuesday and Friday afternoons for five weeks. Meetings in the sixth week were used to prepare for a beginning project. It took two more weeks to complete the project, which involved students tape recording some brief interviews with other students and teachers. Supervisory meetings were also a part of the implementation of the project. Thus, eight weeks passed before the facilitators moved on for more training and some intermediate projects.

Training could be intensified and compressed into one-day "marathon" meetings. While this has the advantage of expediting the training, it makes it more difficult for students to assimilate the ideas and to practice the skills at their own pace.

**Age Level.** Age level can also affect the rate at which students move through training and the kind of projects they undertake. The training sessions that follow are designed primarily for upper grade elementary school students. The reading level of *Becoming a Friendly Helper* is about fifth grade. However, there are some younger students who will also be able to participate (e.g. third and fourth grade). Even though primary grade children can learn some of the concepts and skills, and participate in beginning projects, training sessions would require modifications.

**Vocabulary.** As students proceed through training, they will progressively learn more concepts and skills. They will acquire a helping relationship vocabulary. Some words may appear to be difficult for children, but experience suggests that they enjoy using the "big words." Here are some words that students will learn which conceptualize the helping process and helper roles.

facilitators
communicate
Friendly Helper
helping characteristics
caring
accepting
understanding
trustworthy
careful listener
pleasant and unpleasant feelings
helping responses
open and closed questions
clarifying and summarizing statements

feeling-focused responses
problem-solving model
feedback
feedback model
complimenting
confronting
self-image
Friendly Helper roles
student assistant
tutor
special friend
small group leader

**Student Participation.** It is assumed that the trainees will become more friendly and helpful to one another as they proceed through the training. Most of the experiences and activities encourage students to act positively toward each other, understand each other more, and experience the helping conditions in the training group.

There may be times, however, when a particular student, for whatever reason, might feel uneasy about the lessons or perhaps one part of them. For example, for some reason or another, a student may hesitate to share some ideas. Or, someone may feel self-conscious about a question or activity. The trainer should be alert to these situations and emphasize that any student can "pass" on a given task. Students are not forced to take part.

However, if resistance occurs regularly then it might be best to explore the situation with the student or group. In the event that a student feels uncomfortable because of something that has happened in the group, seize upon the opportunity to review and think about the helping conditions (e.g. trust). Students cannot help but learn from each other, regardless of the circumstances.

## Organization of the Training Sessions

The twenty training sessions are organized along a similar format for your convenience. They are also grouped together by chapters in *Becoming a Friendly Helper,* the student book (See Table 5.1).

*Chapter Highlights* give you a short summary of the related reading in the companion student book.

*Guidelines for Training* are included for each chapter. Thereafter, each session is outlined in terms of its focus, some suggested opening or introductory remarks, ideas for beginning an activity, and hints about presenting the concepts. There is a sequence of events with time allotments, depending upon a 30 or 45 minute period.

*Review Questions* are available for each chapter (*BFH*) rather than for each session. This provides an overview and summary of the basic concepts.

*Supplemental Activities* for each chapter are also included in this book. What follows is designed as an outline from which to work with a minimum of preparation.

**Table 5.1**
**Summary of Training Sessions**

| | BFH Chapter | Training Session | Title | BFH Pages |
|---|---|---|---|---|
| Beginning | 1 | 1 | Friendly Helpers | 1-13 |
| | | 2 | Helping Characteristics | 14-20 |
| | 2 | 3 | Skills for Listening | 21-28 |
| | | 4 | More Listening Skills | 29-34 |
| | 3 | 5 | Looking at Responding | 35-45 |
| | | 6 | Asking Open Questions | 46-49 |
| | | 7 | Clarifying and Summarizing | 50-52 |
| | | 8 | Feeling-focused Responses | 53-57 |
| | | 9 | Looking at the Helping Process | 58-60 |
| | | 10 | Preparing for Beginning Projects | |
| Phases Intermediate | 4 | 11 | Problems, Problems, Problems | 61-69 |
| | | 12 | The Problem Solving Model: Case of Kevin | 70-76 |
| | | 13 | Reviewing the Model | 76-78 |
| | 5 | 14 | The Feedback Model | 79-87 |
| | | 15 | Complimenting and Confronting | 87-90 |
| Advanced | 6 | 16 | Your Self Image | 91-101 |
| | | 17 | Looking at Yourself | 102-110 |
| | | 18 | Putting It All Together | |
| | 7 | 19 | Four Roles and Some Helping Moments | 111-116 |
| | | 20 | Getting Ready to Help Others | 117-119 |

## Orientation

Before you begin the training sessions, you will probably meet with the selected students for one or more orientation meetings. These meetings help you get organized and make the best use of the training sessions.

### Chapter Highlights

There is no corresponding chapter in the student book for orientation to your program. You will structure the meeting(s) based upon contingencies in your school. However, there are some things you may want to consider.

### Guidelines for Orientation

**I. Purpose of the Program.** Although you may have told students individually what you had in mind for the group, you might begin by discussing the group's purpose, some of your expectations, and perhaps some brief glimpses of projects that lie ahead. This is a time to share your enthusiasm. Offer them a challenge.

**II. Operational Procedures.** This is also the time to talk about the "mechanics" of the program and you will meet, duration of the meetings, the number of sessions, arrangements with teachers, contracts, the use of the student book, and so forth. For the most part, these details will focus upon getting the students to the next meeting on time and prepared to work. Other procedures can be explained as you move through the training sessions.

Explaining the operational procedures may not require much time, depending upon the groundwork that has already been laid and the cooperation of the faculty. It will be discouraging if some of the students don't show for your first training session because they didn't obtain permission to attend, were unsure of the meeting place, or arrived late because they forgot. However, if such problems are not of concern then you may choose to use the rest of an orientation meeting for introductions.

**III. Introductions.** Introductions are important to any group. They should not be taken for granted, even if the group members have had some previous acquaintance. For instance, students may be able to call each other by name. They may even know a little about each other from being in a class together, but too many times this is the exception. Therefore, have the students introduce themselves, telling the name that they want to be called, and describing something about themselves.

There are various ways to have introductions. It is very effective when students pair up, interview each other for about 2-3 minutes each and then introduce one another to the group. They can try to learn something that they didn't know before. If desired, you can structure the interviews and introductions for specific information that would be helpful, interesting, or appropriate.

Some topics which students might find interesting are: "What do you think about travel in outer space?" "What is one change that you would make, if you were president of the United States?" "Who would you want to talk with, if you could visit with anyone in the world?" Such topics are fun, as well as informative, and start the group on a stimulating note. You can also play some "name games" where students practice learning and repeating group members' names. This kind of attention early in the first session emphasizes that the group is going to be personal and will value the contributions of each one.

**IV. Student Reactions.** Take time for reactions from students. They will have some questions about the program and the training sessions. Some will ask about goals and projects. Others may express concerns about their abilities. "What makes you think kids will talk with us?" "What if our friends think we are trying to be big-shots?" "How can you help a person who doesn't care?" Still others may reflect some basic insecurities about self. "Are you sure I can do it?" "Are there going to be any tests?" "Will we get a grade?"

As soon as the members show that they have some understanding and are willing to be a part of the group, then you can make the final arrangements and announcements about the first training session.

Student anxiety is reduced as the program is unfolded and as they become more involved, instead of just talking about it. However, a "pep talk," just before you start, settles well with most students. Here are some questions that might help put matters in focus:

1. Who can summarize in a few words what this program is about?
2. Who can tell us something about what some people in the group said about themselves?
3. When are we meeting again?
4. What is something that is still on your mind about the program?
5. What did you hear today that you liked?
6. Is there anything you need before we meet again?

**V. Assignment of Books and Materials.** This might also be an appropriate time to assign the student book, *Becoming a Friendly Helper.* Some students will be so eager to read the book that it may be necessary to tell them not to rush, but to proceed through the book as a training group. The reading assignments are not long or difficult. Even if some students read ahead, the training sessions are arranged so that nothing is lost. Giving students their own book enables them to mark the pages, take notes, and personalize the materials. If other arrangements must be made, now is the time to explain them.

**VI. Reading Assignment.** If everything appears to be in order and if you are ready to start the training sessions, then assign the Introduction and pp. 1-13 *BFH* for "homework."

## Sessions One and Two
## Friendly Helpers and Helping Characteristics

These two sessions start the concept and skill building part of the training. They help students understand the meaning of some terms associated with the program and some fundamental ideas about the helping process.

### Chapter I Highlights *(BFH)*

This chapter begins with a story about Sam, a young boy who receives help from Angie, a student facilitator. *"A student facilitator is someone who uses communication skills to help others talk about ideas and feelings and assists them to make responsible decisions."* The term "friendly helper" is used interchangeably with student or peer facilitator. Some ideas as to what the book is about and how it might be used are included.

Everyone has problems and there is a need for more friendly helpers. Activity 1.1 encourages students to think of a time when they noticed someone who needed help. In Activity 1.2 students explore their preferences for particular helpers given different situations.

The remaining part of this chapter focuses upon four helping characteristics: *caring, accepting, understanding and being trustworthy.* Activity 1.3 motivates students to think about feeling words that describe what people experience. It prepares them for the next chapter.

**Guidelines for Training**

**Session One: Friendly Helpers (pp. 1-13 *BFH*).**

This is your first training session with the students. Introduce them to the need for student facilitators and the term "Friendly Helper." You may prefer a different name and it would be appropriate to use it here. It is best to rely on one term or title to identify the facilitators or helpers (e.g. "friendly helpers," "peer patrols," "student facilitators," or "special buddies." The name is less important than the helping skills and concepts that are taught. As Shakespeare once said, "A rose by any other name is just as sweet." Your task is to focus upon nurturing the sweetness.

**I.** (15-20 minutes) Begin this session with a "warm-up activity." It can help the group members to know each other better and create a feeling of togetherness. It also gives you a chance to model some of the skills students will be learning (e.g. clarifying, responding to feelings).

First, have the students sit in a circle. Then say, "Friendship means a lot of things to different people. Let's go around the circle, with each person taking a turn. Tell what you look for in a friend—what makes a good friend?" Students think about relationships and the topic is one that all can share without study or preparation.

This kind of *go-around activity* will be used in some other sessions too. It is most effective if you: 1) put the students in a close circle, without a table or other barriers in front of them; 2) use the "go-around" to encourage each student to talk and be heard, rather than letting one or two dominate a discussion; 3) proceed from the left (or right) around the circle so that they know when it is their turn to respond to the task or question posed; 4) model the helping responses for the students; and 5) take a turn yourself and share some of your own thoughts on the same task or question.

From the beginning the group will be building trust and cohesiveness. The Orientation Meeting is more of an organizational than a training session. But, in this session the group is on its way. As you model the high facilitative responses, it won't take long before the students realize that is a different group from almost any other that they may have been in. It will be a positive difference that they will like.

**II.** (10-15 minutes) After the warm-up activity and if students have already read pages 1-12 *(BFH),* then you might say, "In the story about Sam and Angie, what happened?" Listen for comments about the helping process and how Angie went about being friendly. Then, ask the group, "Angie was a student facilitator. That's a big word. What does it mean (p. 3)?"

Reach an understanding that everyone has problems and conflicts in life. The other examples in the book will help. Emphasize that there is nothing wrong with having a problem. Friendly helpers can assist people to make responsible decisions and resolve problems.

**III.** (5-10 minutes) You can conclude this session with Activity 1.1 (p. 13) "Who Needs Help?" Or, this can be used as a homework and outside assignment. The person in the picture can be anonymous. Tell the students that their art work is not as important as drawing a picture that can be used to tell a story. Assign Activity 1.2 (p. 14) "Who Are The Helpers." Ask them to read the rest of the chapter (pp. 15-19) and complete Activity 1.3 (p. 20) "Feeling Word Search." This is a fun activity where students search for feeling words. It is the first of several activities that help each student build a "feelings word" vocabulary.

## Session Two: The Helping Characteristics (pp. 14-20 *BFH*)

This session is about different helpers and four helping characteristics. While students can go to many people for help, emphasize that students can be helpers too. "By learning some special skills you can be a friendly helper and give more help than you ever have before."

**I.** (10-15 minutes) "Share and tell" time, as a follow-up to Activity 1.1, is optional, depending upon time. However, you will probably want to begin with Activity 1.2.

Activity 1.2 starts the group thinking about different helpers. You could begin by saying, "Let's go around the circle and see which helper on the list had the most lines and symbols." "Now, let's go around again. This time tell how many lines and symbols were used for *friendly students?*" "What do you and others look for when you want some help?"

**II.** (15-20 minutes) Have the group discuss the four helping characteristics: caring, accepting, understanding and being trustworthy.

These four characteristics were selected from many that could be used. You could add more. It seems adviseable, however, that these be added as they emerge from discussions and experiential activities with the students. Otherwise, they will complicate matters at this point. Almost all the other helping characteristics described in the professional literature can be related to these four.

Being committed is often linked with the concept of "caring." Caring enough to take interest and get involved is the essence of the work in a peer program. Accepting people for what they are as human beings, wihout necessarily accepting their behavior is a more difficult concept and may need additional attention.

Training Student Facilitators

"People do the best they can and we want to help them do better if they are having problems." The keys to understanding are described. Being trustworthy emphasizes the importance of respecting the rights and privacy of someone, but it translates most easily to students as "I trust that you will not hurt me with what I tell you." This is different than emphasizing confidentiality. Confidentiality seems a less desirable term than "being trusted or being trustworthy."

A few trainers may want their students to learn the helping characteristic words to the point that everything else is secondary (and perhaps unnecessary). Yet, later chapters will help students discuss and learn specific things that they can do to be perceived as a helping person. Because it is impossible to teach all the skills and behaviors associated with the helping process, it is important for students to know the characteristics that they are trying to develop for themselves and create with others.

II (5-10 minutes) Conclude this session with the chapter review questions. You might also check Activity 1.3 (p. 20). This is an introductory experience to "feeling words."

Assign pp. 21-28 *(BFH)*, including Activity 2.1 (p . 24) "Feeling Faces—Part I" and Activity 2.2 (pp. 27-28) "Key Words and Feelings."

**Review Questions for Chapter I:**
1. What is a friendly helper? A student facilitator?
2. What does it mean to be caring? Accepting? Understanding? Trustworthy?
3. Who can be a friendly helper or student facilitator?
4. Who can benefit from a friendly helper?
5. What is the difference between someone who is just a good friend and a student facilitator? Can you be both?

## Sessions Three and Four
## The Careful Listener

Sessions Three and Four help students to improve their skills in listening. Careful listening is basic to effective communication. Facilitators need to improve their listening abilities before proceeding to other helping skills.

## Chapter II Highlights *(BFH)*

Being a careful listener is an important skill for learning. It is essential for making and keeping friends, succeeding in school, and being an effective friendly helper. Listening is more than just hearing words. To listen carefully, facilitators must keep four things in mind.

1. *Look at the person who is talking.* "Good eye contact can show caring." Activity 2.1 gives students practice in seeing what others are feeling.

2. *Pay attention to the person's words.* "Listen for the main ideas and remember a few key words." In Activity 2.2, students practice picking out main topics and feelings.

3. *Be aware of a person's feelings.* "Feelings are part of everyone and can be viewed as either pleasant or unpleasant." Lists of feeling words are presented in Table 1. In Activity 2.3, students differentiate pleasant from unpleasant feeling words. In Activity 2.4, they identify feeling words.

4. *Say something that shows you are listening.* "A careful listener shows the talker that the listener is understanding and interested by telling what was heard."

## Guidelines for Training

### Session Three: Skills for Listening (pp. 21-28 *BFH*)

This session focuses on listening and two of the four guidelines for careful listening. Although students are often told to be better listeners, they are rarely given practice in specific skills.

**I.** (10-15 minutes) Start the session by asking the students to look at the statements made by teachers who are concerned about listening (p. 21). "Which ones sound familiar?" "Can you add more to the list?" "Were any of these statements heard recently?" "What do students do that cause teachers to say these things?" Then, have the students share some of their experiences with poor listening.

This can lead to an interesting discussion. "Careful listening is more than just being quiet and hearing someone's words. It takes special concentration. It is a skill that we can all improve upon—adults too. It is also a basic skill for student facilitators. All the rest of the skills that you will be taught in the book depend upon your listening abilities."

**II.** (10-15 minutes) Discuss Activity 2.1 (p. 24) "Feeling Faces— Part I." This activity is about the first listening skill, *"Look at the person who is talking."* Students practice reading facial expressions. It serves as an example of how faces can give us more information about people than just words.

Solution to Activity 2.1 "Feeling Faces—Part I" (pp. 24-25)

Face A:
excited
(sad)
relaxed

Face B:
shocked
joyful
(bored)

Face C:
cheerful
(unsure)
angry

Face D:
(fascinated)
frustrated
afraid

Face E:
terrified
(nervous)
calm

Face F:
confused
(angry)
grateful

Children Helping Children

**III.** (5-10 minutes) Use Activity 2.2 (pp. 27-28) "Key Words and Feelings" to focus on the second skill of listening, *"Pay attention to the person's words."* The activity gives students practice in identifying central ideas and feelings.

Here are the best choices for the cases:

**Case 1 (Danny).** The key idea is No. 5, "You don't like what Jim did." The other four answers are not supported in what Danny said. The best word which describes his feeling is No. 3, "Angry." Though Danny might be feeling some of the other feelings too, his statements clearly show his anger toward Jim.

**Case 2 (Suzanne).** The key idea is No. 1, "You are thinking a lot about the test." The other four answers may be true, but they can only be guessed from what Suzzane said. The best word which describes her feeling is No. 4, "Worried."

If time permits, tell the students about something that you experienced while on vacation. Ask the group to write the key words that capture the main ideas. What feeling words describe your experience? You might tell of two more events just for practice.

**IV.** End this session by reminding students that sorting out and recalling main ideas from a person's conversation is a valuable skill that can be used in a lot of places. Think of examples. For instance, sometimes students have a difficult time remembering directions given by teachers and parents. "Careful listening is a skill that can be practiced each day in a lot of places."

Assign pp. 29-34 *(BFH),* including Activity 2.3 (p. 31) "Feeling Faces—Part II" and Activity 2.4 (p. 32)"The Lunchroom Line."

### Session Four: More Listening Skills (pp. 29-34 *BFH*).

This session gives students two more skills in careful listening. Special attention is on building a feeling word vocabulary, including a focus on *pleasant and unpleasant feelings*. Most students lack a feeling word vocabulary. They don't hear the words very often in school or at home. Yet, with more extensive feeling word vocabularies they can communicate better.

**I.** (10-15 minutes) You might begin by saying, "Turn to page 31 and Activity 2.3. Let's look at each picture and the feeling words. Which words did you mark as pleasant? Unpleasant?" This could lead to a discussion of Table 1.

**II.** (10-15 minutes) Now, have the students look at the picture on p. 32 Activity 2.4 (The Lunchroom Line). Discuss what is taking place in the picture. There are no right or wrong interpretations. Note that different feeling words could be correct for each group of boys and girls, depending upon different interpretations of what is happening. Here are some possible answers:

Group 1 (the boys standing)

> Embarassed
> Disgusted
> Angry
> Annoyed
> Picked-on
> (others?)

Group 2 (the two girls)

> Pleased
> Strong
> Amused
> Enjoyment
> Pleased
> (other?)

In addition to the activities in the student book and the supplemental activities in this book, there are several things that you might do to help students learn more about feelings and develop a better feeling word vocabulary. Here are some possible in-and out-of-session activities or assignments:

— Include feeling words in classroom spelling assignments.

— Have students compile lists of feeling words from their classroom reading assignments.

— Have them identify feeling words from a story, play, movie or television program.

— Have the students circle ten words from Table 1 that can be new words to learn and practice using.

— While one student briefly describes an experience, others listen for feelings and write words to describe them.

— Have students identify feeling words which describe emotions expressed in music or art work.

— Have them draw pictures or chose colors which represent different feelings.

— Feelings may be pantomimed by the group members. Role play situations which illustrate feelings.

— A feeling word game could be put together by you or the students, for example, a roll-the-dice board game in which players advance around a path that is full of spaces with directions. Some spaces ask the player to draw a card. These cards might contain feeling words. When a player draws a card, that player must pantomime or tell a story while the others try to guess the feeling.

— Students may compete with each other to see who can name or list the most feeling words in two minutes.

**III.** (10-15 minutes) Use the last part of the session to talk about the last of the four listening skills, *"Say something that shows you are listening."* You might start the discussion with something like this, "To show that you are really listening and understanding what is being said, say something. But, what can you say or do?" Clarify their responses and give particular attention to those that emphasize a helping response. Then say, "We will find some more ways in Chapter III *(BFH)* and talk about them in our next four sessions." Conclude the session with the chapter review questions.

Assign pp. 35-45 *(BFH)*. There are no specific activities. There are, however, cases which require their responses.

### Review Questions for Chapter II

1. Why is listening so important to friendly helping?
2. What are four things that careful listeners do?
3. Why is it helpful to look at the person who is talking with you?
4. What are three new feeling words that you learned?
5. What is the difference between pleasant and unpleasant feelings?
6. Is it wrong to have unpleasant feelings?
7. What feeling words from Table 1 do you find the most interesting and the most unusual?

## Sessions Five, Six, Seven, and Eight
## Making Helpful Responses

Training sessions Five, Six, Seven, and Eight provide ideas and practice of verbal responses that are essential to the work of friendly helpers. It is not enough for students to want to help. They must have some listening and communication skills in order to facilitate others to think about their ideas and feelings. Note that the "Pass the Pencil" activity, on pages 260-261, has been found by program coordinators to be particularly useful in teaching these skills.

### Chapter III Highlights *(BFH)*

Students become more aware of what they can say in response to others. The cases of Paul and Jeanne as well as Diane and Joe, offer opportunities to pre-test communication skills and to identify different kinds of helping statements. Three high facilitative responses are presented: 1) open questions; 2) clarifying and summarizing; and 3) feeling-focused statements.

### Guidelines for Training

### Session Five: Looking at Responding (pp. 35-45 *BFH*)

The cases of Jeanne and Paul are used in this session to help students identify different kinds of statements that might be made in a helping relationship. Students first make some open-ended responses. They then select favored responses from some possibilities. The possible impact of their choices is explored. Finally, students rank order some response choices in the cases of Diane and Joe. This session is an assessment of responding tendencies as well as an introduction to making more helpful responses.

**I.** (10-15 minutes) Start this session by saying, "Let's look at the cases you have been working on. Turn to the case of Jeanne (p. 36) and let's take turns telling the responses that we wrote." After each one reports ask, "What were you trying to do?" or "What were you hoping that you would accomplish with your response?" Next, look at the case of Paul and do the same thing. Also have the students share the words that they used to describe Jeanne's feelings.

**II.** (10-15 minutes) In a second set of responses, to the cases of Jeanne and Paul, students select favored response from some choices. Discuss their choices and other statements. In the case of Paul, students are asked to specifically focus on a feeling response.

**III.** (10-15 minutes) The cases of Dianne and Joe give students an opportunity to rank possible responses and compare themselves to effective responses given by other student facilitators. More discussion takes place regarding choices, the different kinds of responses made, and their "probable impact." This should motivate students to want more information about the helping responses that are introduced in the next three sessions.

You may want to develop your own inventory to use as a pre-test of different responses, including some more hypothetical situations. This not only helps you learn the communication habits or tendencies of students at this point, but could also be used as a measure of progress later in the program when a similar post-test is given. (See Chapter VII of this book).

Assign pp. 46-49 *(BFH)* including Activity 3.1 (p. 49) "Questioning A Friend."

**Session Six: Asking Open Questions (pp. 46-53 *BFH*)**

Helping responses are introduced beginning with open and closed questions in this session. Open and closed questions can both be helpful at times. However, closed questions usually require less input by the respondent and when taken literally they stifle the communication process. The goal is to encourage students to use more open questions.

**I.** (10-15 minutes) Begin the session by asking, "What is the difference between a closed and an open question?" Clarify the differences by reviewing the examples on pp. 46-51. Then, say something like this, "Now, let's see how these questions can be used with a topic. What did you write as examples to the topics on p. 48 (i.e. school and tennis)? After students report their examples and the assignment is discussed, give the following topics as additional practice. Ask the students to give more examples of closed and open questions.

Some Additional Topics:

   Television
   Fish
   Weather
   Pizza

**II.** (10-15 minutes) Activity 3.1 (p. 49) "Questioning a Friend" follows next. Read the instructions aloud and clarify them. If desired, model the procedure first before someone volunteers. This activity is an opportunity for students to practice open and closed questions, share ideas, and be listened to by the group. It also gives practice in identifying the different questions.

**III.** (10-15 minutes) Conclude this session with some more practice. Pair the students and have them take places around the room. Taking turns, one student talks while the other becomes a listener who will ask at least four open questions. After students take their turns, have them talk about the experience— what they liked best and least. If there is an odd number of students, the trainer might pair with a student and practice too— taking a turn as described.

Assign pp. 50-52 *(BFH)*. The activities for the chapter will be completed during the next session.

### Session Seven: Clarifying and Summarizing (pp. 50-52 *BFH*)

This session is about clarifying and summarizing responses. They are similar in that each concentrates upon ideas and events that were expressed. Whereas feeling responses, discussed in the next session, tend to create more excitement and intensity, these responses are generally more comforting because they do not communicate at such a deep level of understanding.

You may not find it necessary to explain the subtle differences between clarifying and summarizing. However, here are a few for your information. Clarifying tends to focus upon one idea and might be used when a helper is unsure about something that the helpee has said. Why go on with the conversation if there is some misunderstanding or doubt in the mind of the facilitator? Then again, the facilitator may have heard the words and understood them but wants to clarify anyway. The intent is to deliberately bring attention to some words, events, or ideas expressed by the helpee.

Summarizing, on the other hand, is usually intended as way of capsulizing a few ideas that have been expressed. As a response, it collects important ideas that are emerging and centers them for discussion. Or, it can be helpful as a response to tie or link ideas together.

**I.** (5 minutes) Begin this session by asking, "What does a clarifying and summarizing response do?" "How are they different from a question?" "Is there any value in repeating back ideas, even though you might already be sure of what the person said?" What is the difference between clarifying and parroting words?"

**II.** (10-15 minutes) Activity 3.2 (p. 52) "Clarifying and Summarizing Ideas" helps students practice the responses. It is similar to Activity 3.1 in that it is also a "go around." Students take turns sharing something about themselves while others practice responding to them. Again, this is not a role playing situation. Students tell something that has really happened to them, or something that they are thinking about.

Read the directions aloud (p. 52) and begin. Encourage them to be patient with each other, as they take their time to think of and make responses. This is a practice session. Later, they may pick up the speed at which they respond, which would keep a conversation running smoother.

After everyone has had a turn, you might say something like this: "Last session we practiced asking open questions. This time our clarifying responses showed that we were listening and following the ideas and events that were being talked about. Questions and clarifying or summarizing can be a helpful team of responses."

**III.** (10-20 minutes) Now, divide the group into pairs as you did in the previous session. You may want to pair them so that they have different partners this time. Again, the students will take turns being a "talker" and a "facilitator." The talker can begin by sharing something that has happened to them recently at home or school. Or, the following and similar topics might be used to help them talk about something for this activity:

Some possible topics:

A dream I had
My favorite food
A time when I made a mistake
A time when I was proud of myself
Something that bothers me
One change I'd like to see in the school
One complaint I have about adults
My favorite music
A vacation I'd like to have
What I would do with 1,000 dollars

Then say, "Each of you will get a chance to be a talker and a facilitator. The talker will say something and the facilitator will first ask an open question. After the question is answered by the talker the facilitator then makes a clarifying or summarizing response. In other words, the facilitator asks a question, the talker responds, and then the facilitator makes a clarifying response."

In a second round, students switch roles again. A new topic is introduced. However, this time the facilitator's task is to ask at least two questions and make at least two clarifying or summarizing statements before ending a turn. This is good practice in helping to keep a conversation going and keeping the focus on someone who is talking. This is "limited" practice and there is no attempt to solve someone's problem, if it should arise. Sometimes the topic is so stimulating that students want to continue.

**IV.** (5 minutes) End this session by asking the students how they felt about what they learned and practiced. This will give you an idea of whether or not a supplementary activity is needed before proceeding to feeling-focused responses. It is important that students not be rushed. They learn best through small progressive steps.

A "homework" assignment could be: "Use your knowledge of clarifying with someone. Clarify someone's ideas before we meet next time. Remember to use fresh words when you clarify or summarize what you heard them say."

Assign pp. 53-57, Activity 3.3 will be done during the next session.

## Session Eight: Feeling-focused Responses (pp. 53-57 *BFH*).

This session emphasizes the use of the "feeling-focused response." For children it is a response that is seldom modeled by adults. Most adults have not had an opportunity to learn it.

**I.** (5 minutes) Begin by saying something like this, "Today we are going to learn more about a very important skill in listening. It is perhaps the most effective skill in telling others that you are really trying to understand them. This response goes beyond the words that a person says to you. It focuses upon what the person is feeling. What are some things that have happened around school where you noticed people's feelings?" As students share their experiences, ask them, "Was that a pleasant or unpleasant feeling—or both?" This helps them slow down and tune-in. It will provide them some structure for being aware of feelings when they talk with others.

Some trainers like to build their own feeling-word lists with the help of their students. Using tag board, newsprint or perhaps construction paper, feeling words can be recorded and posted somewhere in the room for easy reference.

**II.** (10-15 minutes) Activity 3.3 (p. 57) "Feeling-Focused Responses" is another go around experience in which students use the now familiar format of sharing an idea and practicing a response.

**III.** (10-20 minutes) After students have completed the Activity 3.3, divide them into pairs. Again, you may want to put them into different pairs than before. If you have a target student in the group who is receiving "training as treatment" then you will probably give more consideration to the pairing, perhaps deliberately pairing the target child with another of your choice.

Then say, "Now it's time to put all three of our helping responses to work. Last time we asked questions and clarified responses. This time we will add the feeling-focused response. Here is your task: The talker begins by sharing some ideas. The facilitator may use any one of the three helping responses we discussed. However, keep the conversation going until all three responses have been made at least once. You may feel a little awkward at first, but remember that we are practicing this together and you will get better. Okay, begin."

**IV.** (5 minutes) After both students have taken a turn, have them talk about the experience. Conclude by asking some of the chapter review questions.

Ask the students to review Chapter III and complete Activity 3.4 (pp. 58-59) "Following Charlie's Talk."

**Review Questions for Chapter III**
1. What is it that makes some responses more facilitative than others?
2. What kinds of responses do most people make when they talk to one another? Listen for them at home, on the school ground and in class.
3. Describe three responses that can be used by friendly helpers or student facilitators.
4. Of what value is it to summarize someone's ideas?
5. Why don't we hear more statements responding to people's feelings in our everyday life?
6. Of all the possible responses, which one seems to show the most understanding of a person?
7. What happens when a facilitator asks only questions? Gives only feeling responses?
8. What makes us feel awkward when we are first learning to make feeling responses?

## Session Nine

## Looking at the Helping Process

This session is an opportunity to review the concepts and skills learned to this point. It can be an opportunity to assess student progress. You will learn if they need more practice before starting some beginning projects.

## Chapter Highlights

Since this is a review and assessment session, *BFH* Chapters I, II, and III are relevant. The key concepts and skills outlined previously are given attention.

## Guidelines for Training

### Session Nine: Looking at the Helping Process (pp. 58-60 *BFH*)

**I.** (5-10 minutes) The case of Charlie and Activity 3.4 in this session, provides a summary experience for ideas in Chapter III. Students identify the responses (p.58) and complete the dot-to-dot picture (p. 59). As a follow-up you could make up some more illustrations of the helping responses. Ask the students to listen as you say them. Have them identify the kind of response that you are giving. They might also make up similar responses to the ones you give, but use different words. Such variations will give them more practice and tell you how integrated their learning has been.

**II.** (20-25 minutes) Some role-playing experiences can be used for additional practice and assessment. Describe some situations. Ask students to take turns acting them out, while the rest of the group watches and listens. The observers might take notes for later comments and suggestions. Encourage them to look for the positive things that the helpers do in the situation.

Some possible role-playing situations are:

A. A new student has arrived at school. It's lunchtime and the person is looking around, appearing unsure where to go. What will you do and say?

B. A girl (or boy) comes to school crying and she is missing her shoe. What now?

C. Two children are arguing over a ball. You are worried that it could turn into a fight.

D. A teacher has mistakenly accused a child of doing something. You saw what happened. What can you do when you talk with the child? The teacher?

E. A boy (or girl) received a merit award for penmanship. He seems surprised.

F. As you are assisting a teacher put up a bulletin board, the teacher rubs her head and says she has an awful headache.

G. You have been helping a second grade student with addition and subtraction. It is something that the person doesn't want to do and there is a lot of complaining.

H. Two students are teasing a younger student. They are laughing, while the young person is getting frustrated. The two want you to join in "the fun." What would you say to the two students later when you had a chance to talk about the experience. What about the young person?

**III.** (5-10 minutes) Conclude this session with the review questions. Any other remarks to prepare them for the next session — "Preparing for a Beginning Project" — would be appropriate.

**Review Questions for Chapters I, II, and III**

1. Of all the responses, which one seems most difficult to practice in our sessions? Outside our meetings?

2. What is the value of making a feeling-focused response instead of an open-ended question?

3. Think of a situation that happened in school today when a feeling-focused response might have been appropriate. What happened? What kept that person from receiving such a response? What would you say if it happened again?

4. What do you like best about what we've done in our training sessions so far? What have you liked least?

5. What more do you need before you could be more facilitative of:

    a) A student you are tutoring

    b) An adult visitor to the school

    c) A friend who wants to talk with you

    d) A small group you are leading

## Session Ten

## Preparing For Beginning Projects

Student facilitator training is not complete at this point. There are still other skills to be learned before a facilitator will feel confident in various roles. However, this is a point where students might engage in some beginning projects and where they can practice their new skills. Some beginning projects are suggested in Chapter VI of this book.

## Chapter Highlights

There is no corresponding chapter for this session in the student book. Although it is the concluding chapter, there are parts of Chapter VII *(BFH)* which might be relevant now. For example, possible roles and functions (pp. 111-114) might be summarized for them.

## Guidelines for Training
### Session Ten: Preparing for Beginning Projects.

**I.** (30-45 minutes) Students prepare for a project in this session. In a beginning project, roles and functions are more limited. Select a structured experience for the students, one in which they know their role and have a clear idea of the tasks. For example, the Gainesville Project, described on pp. 204-206, was part of a beginning program. The tasks and helping responses were designed ahead of time and each student facilitator practiced leading the facilitator group to learn what was expected and what might happen.

Some beginning projects are more successful if the functions, tasks, and activities in the project have been practiced in training sessions. For example, interviewing a parent and using the helping skills is limited in scope and might be appropriate. Likewise, the facilitators could be small group discussion leaders, as in the Gainesville Project (Chapter VI). Role-playing and simulations can help the students to become more familiar with their projects. For example, in the Gainesville Project, the tasks and helping responses were designed ahead of time and each student facilitator practiced leading the facilitator group to learn what was expected and what might happen.

Avoid putting students in situations where they have to be more skillful than what they are at this time. For instance, they haven't yet focused upon problem-solving and decision-making. While they can be of some help to students who are having problems and while they can use the helping responses to take a person-centered approach, they might feel at a loss when it comes to helping some persons. Likewise, feedback—complimenting and confronting—are skills still to be learned. Therefore, this may not be a time to have them in projects where they are helping to set limits with disruptive students. That can come later.

Here are some questions that might help you select a beginning project. At what skill level are the students? What kind of project would help them feel successful? Would it be better to have them work with others in a small group or individually? Should students work together as co-leaders or on their own? What basic skills and tasks are needed to accomplish the project? When should the project start? How long should it last? (See Chapter VI).

Use the session to describe the project, the facilitator roles and functions, and any procedures that must be followed. Role-play certain tasks. Use simulations for anticipated situations. Model beginning and closing steps. Clarify goals and review expectations.

If an additional session is needed as part of preparation, then it might be arranged at this time. Otherwise, have students begin the project, and use subsequent sessions to explore results and provide supervision.

Upon completion of the project, students proceed through the remaining training sessions, beginning with Chapter IV *(BFH)*. Assign pp. 61-69 including Activity 4.1 "Students Have Problems Too."

## Sessions Eleven, Twelve, and Thirteen
### Helping Solve Problems

These three sessions help students learn how to solve problems through responsible decision-making. Problem-solving can help people find solutions and take action. Facilitators can be more helpful if they are trained in the problem-solving model.

### Chapter IV Highlights (*BFH*)

While some problems are more serious than others, they are a part of everyday living. Everyone has problems. Problems "stir us up" with unpleasant feelings and we must work on them before we can feel "settled again." Problems are challenges. Sometimes, it is tedious work to find ways to resolve them.

*A five-step problem solving model is described.* The five steps are based on questions that can be asked. These can lead someone to make more responsible decisions.

1. What is the problem?
2. What have you tried?
3. What else could you do and what would happen?
4. What is your next step?
5. How did it go?

In the case of Kevin, students work through each step and some possible responses.

## Guidelines for Training

### Session Eleven: Problems, Problems, Problems (pp. 61-69).

Students begin their intermediate training phase with a focus upon the nature of problems. Session eleven helps them realize that everyone has problems and that problems can be challenges. The first step is to identify problems and be aware of the feelings that often accompany them. In addition, students examine problems that face young people.

**I.** (5 minutes) Begin the session by discussing the case of Deborah. "What are some feelings that Deborah is having in this situation? What would you do?"

**II.** (10-15 minutes) Then, ask the students to think some more about Activity 4.1 (p. 67). This activity is designed to help students realize that there are many kinds of problems that students their age could experience. Some are more serious than others. Some are a result of someone else having a problem. But, all of the problems have unpleasant feelings associated with them. Using the list in Activity 4.1 select some problems of interest and have the students brainstorm 1) feelings that might accompany the problem and 2) some initial helping responses that could be made.

It is not necessary for students to reveal a personal problem for discussion in the session. That might be too threatening or take too much time from the lesson. However, it helps to personalize the learning experience by having students think of problems that they know about or have experienced.

**III.** (10-15 minutes) Next, divide the group into smaller groups of two or three. Have the groups list (in 5 minutes) problems that students their age have had or are experiencing. Then, ask the groups to share their lists with the entire group.

The following discussion questions might be relevant.

1. What problems were common to all the lists?
2. Which problems apply to students in the primary grades? To teachers?
3. Which ones might take longer to work out?
4. Which ones are common to girls? To boys? To both?
5. How would you rank order the top three in terms of the most common to students?

**IV.** (5-10 minutes) Conclude the session by reminding them that people often feel reassured when they know that others have problems too or that they are not the only ones with problems. Ask them, however, how a person would feel if someone said the following:

- "Oh, everyone has problems like that, you aren't the only one, you know."
- "Don't worry, everything will work out."
- "Nobody's perfect."

While these reassuring and supportive statements might feel good at first, help students realize that they are not helpful statements because they dismiss a person's feelings or ignore them.

Assign pp. 70-76 *(BFH)*. Students work through the case of Kevin as they learn the five-step problem solving model.

### Session Twelve: The Problem-Solving Model: Case of Kevin (pp. 70-76 *BFH*)

Through the Case of Kevin, students learn and practice the five steps of the problem-solving model. Continuity of the steps is added if the students can work through the case and the model in this session.

**I.** ( 25-40 minutes) Begin by saying, "Let's look at the Case of Kevin. Turn to page 70." Ask the group members to sit in a semicircle arrangement, with one chair placed in front. Let one of the students sit in the chair and read the part of Kevin, while you read the helping responses. When you get to a place where a student response is called for, stop and ask the group members what they wrote or would say. Not everyone needs to share each time, but everyone should participate in this session. You might want to ask half the group to report what they would say the first time, and then at the next opportunity request the other half to tell their responses.

Keep the session moving, but take time to answer questions and explore ideas when appropriate. Steps 1 and 5 usually take less discussion and stimulate fewer questions than the others.

**II.** (5 minutes) Conclude the session by reviewing the five steps. Ask the students to put the steps to memory for the next session.

Assign the summary and Activity 4.2 (pp. 76-48) "A Problem-Solving Journey." Tell the students that the next session will be used for them to practice the model.

### Session Thirteen: Reviewing the Model (pp. 76-78 *BFH*)

This session is used for practicing the five-step problem-solving model. In addition, students are encouraged to use helping responses within the process of leading someone through the steps.

**I.** (15-20 minutes) Start the session by saying, "Who can remember the five steps or questions of the problem-solving model?" After helping the students to recall the steps, tell them that this session will be used to practice the model in some problem-solving situations.

Then, arrange the chairs in a semicircle again, but this time place two chairs in front of the group. Someone volunteers to be the person with a problem. The problem may be one of the group's choosing or assigned by the trainer. For example, the following might be among those considered. Role-play a student who:

1. is having problems with a class project.
2. is sitting next to someone who is "cheating."
3. believes that some other students are making fun of this student.
4. has lost a watch.
5. has been turned down to be on a school team.
6. says, "I don't have any money to spend."

The volunteer sits in one of the chairs, while the other chair is left open for the "helper." Group members take turns sitting in the helper chair and using the problem-solving model one step at a time. For example, the first helper talks with the volunteer who has the problem until the first step is "complete." Then, a second student takes over and talks with the volunteer. leading the person through the second step of the model. Next, a third student takes the helper chair and proceeds with the third step, and so on until all five steps have been accomplished.

In general, the first problem and rotation of helpers take the most time to complete. Thereafter, students have a better idea of what the tasks are with each step and the process can move a little faster.

Assist students in recalling the steps and the use of the helping responses. Don't let the group get bogged down on any one problem. Repetition of the steps is more productive than working one case in detail. As soon as students have an idea of how a step is used, move on to the next step rather than explore all alternatives or possibilities. Encouragement helps students master the model.

**II.** (10-20 minutes) After students have witnessed one walk-through with the model, divide them into groups of three each. One student talks about a problem (perhaps from the list on p. 137) while a second student plays the helper role and uses the first two steps of the model. The third student observes and offers suggestions before taking over the helper role and going on with steps 3 and 4. The first helper then becomes the observer. Afterwards, students discuss how the fifth step might be used.

This task can be repeated with another problem and with someone else being the volunteer. This gives all students an opportunity to practice with the model.

As the groups are practicing, move from one to the other unless it is necessary for you to be in one group yourself to have a sufficient number. Timely coaching might be offered.

**III.** (5 minutes) End the session by asking the students to share some of their reactions to the experience. "Can you think of times and places where the model might be helpful with others?" "Can you think of a time when the model would have been helpful to you?"

If time allows, ask the chapter review questions. Or, the questions might be used at the beginning of the next session.

Assign pp. 79-87, Chapter IV, *(BFH)*.

**Review Questions for Chapter IV**

1. What are the five steps or questions of the problem-solving model?
2. Why is it important to ask what the person has tried and what else might be done?
3. When is the best time to share your own ideas for solutions?
4. Why ask someone, "How did it go?"
5. Why is it important to ask a person what else could you do and what would happen if you did that?
6. What could you do if the person tells you that the plan didn't work out?
7. How are helping responses learned in Chapter III related to the problem-solving model?

## Sessions Fourteen and Fifteen
### Giving Feedback

Sessions Fourteen and Fifteen help students learn to compliment and confront others about their behavior. Both skills are needed in a comprehensive student facilitator program.

### Chapter V Highlights *(BFH)*

The term "feedback" is used to describe the impact that people are having on us. Most people want feedback, especially if it is timely and given in a caring way. A three-part feedback model is described which facilitators can use in their work with individuals or groups:

1. Be specific about what you see and hear.
2. Tell what you are feeling.
3. Tell what your feelings make you want to do.

Depending upon whether the person using the model is speaking of their pleasant of unpleasant feelings, a compliment or confrontation takes place.

**Guidelines for Training**

**Session Fourteen: The Feedback Model (pp. 79-87 *BFH*)**

A lot of information is presented in this session. It describes the concept of giving feedback and presents a three-step feedback model. The model might be introduced in more than one session, but this tends to break the continuity of learning it. *Trainer notes for the feedback model.* The first step in the feedback model is to describe what is observed—what you see or hear. Encourage students to be specific and give examples that illustrate what they have noticed about the person to whom they are giving feedback. They may need additional practice in observing and taking note of others' behavior. Observing and describing someone's actions might be a useful supplemental activity.

Part two of the model focuses upon the facilitator's feelings— not the feelings of the person who is receiving the feedback. In other words, this is a time when the student facilitator must tune-in to self and be aware of pleasant or unpleasant feelings.

To this point in the training sessions, the major emphasis has been upon listening and responding to the feelings of others. Feedback will be most effective if the facilitator's own reactions are given. Sometimes it will be helpful to say to the students, "Tell what you notice. Okay, now tune into yourself. Are you experiencing pleasant or unpleasant feelings in the presence of that behavior?

Now, what do your feelings make you want to do?" The third part of the model focuses on behavior too—the behavior of the facilitator. While the person receiving the feedback may have triggered some reaction in the facilitator, facilitators are still responsible for their behavior, regardless of the feeling.

Although they are not mentioned in the student book, here are some cautions about the feedback model: 1) Avoid judging a person. For example: "The trouble with you is that you are lazy." Or, "You are a selfish person." These statements are conclusions that have been reached because of what someone has done. Help your students go beyond judgments and labels. 2) Avoid giving advice. Feedback has too often been associated with telling another person what should be done. Sometimes people use all three parts of the feedback model effectively, only to detract from it when they tack on some advice at the end.

Confrontations are a concern to most people. We are afraid that if we confront someone, then that person won't like us anymore. That might be true if the confrontation labels and puts the person down. However, if the feedback model is used, then people often begin to feel closer because the relationship is more open and honest.

Three suggestions about confrontations might be passed on to students. These are not included in the student book: 1) They should spend some time trying to be a careful listener with the person that they want to confront. High facilitative responses lead to increased understanding. If after some listening time is spent and the unpleasant feelings are still present, then also consider the next suggestion. 2) Is this a persistent and recurring feeling that you experience? Does the person continue to "bug" you with the same kind of behavior or action? If so, then perhaps you need to speak up. 3) But, be aware of your choice of words. Some words are too intense or harsh and the person loses the impact of your feedback statement when the words are shocking (e.g. "When you interrupt me while I'm talking, it makes me hate you so much that I want you to drop dead!") Even this kind of intense feeling, however, can be softened and used effectively when the feedback model is used.

**I.** (5 minutes) Begin this session by asking, "What is meant by the term feedback?" Emphasize that they will be learning a three-step feedback model that will help them both compliment and confront others.

**II.** (10-15 minutes) Then, give them some practice in observing behavior. Ask a volunteer to act out a pantomine, although words could be used. This brief scene is observed by group members, who later report what they saw happening. This might be a good opportunity to draw attention to the fact that not everyone sees the same thing or is impressed by the same events.

Next, ask the group members to tell what kind of feelings they experienced as they watched the pantomine or scene that was being acted out. Focus on what the observers were feeling, not what the person acting in the scene was feeling. This important difference is necessary before they can tune-in to themselves and use the second step of the model.

Some possible pantomimes or scenes to act out for this activity might be someone who:

A. is angry or mad at something.
B. is lonely and then is spoken to by someone who is friendly.
C. is sneaking up on someone else.
D. peeks into a box and is surprised.
E. is laughing and pointing at someone else.

**III.** (10-20 minutes) Now, tell the students to turn to p. 86, Review the three parts of the feedback model which were applied to a family member.

Then, ask each group member to read aloud the feedback that they put together on p. 87. This is a powerful activity and all students should report what they wrote, which also gives the trainer an opportunity to do more coaching. In the event that some students' feedback are more personal and they are uncomfortable sharing with the group, have them think of examples that they can share.

**IV.** (5 minutes) End this session by asking the students to think of a time when they might best give the family member the feedback that they practiced , (or something nearly like it). Encourage them to try it out.

Assign pp. 87-90, including Activity 5.1 (p. 87), "Some Feedback to Others." Remind students to write out their examples on a piece of paper that might be collected. Activity 5.2 will be completed during the next session.

### Session Fifteen: Complimenting and Confronting (pp. 87-90)

**I.** (5-10 minutes) Open this session by telling the students to turn to p. 88, "Feedback to Rod." Ask them to look at the different examples again and tell how they are the same and different. Have the students underline part one with a single line, part two with a double line, and part three with three lines. Next, circle the key feeling words expressed in each example. This last effort should help students clearly identify the central difference between a compliment and a confrontation.

**II.** (10 minutes) Then, tell the students to look at Activity 5.1 (p. 87), "Some Feedback to Others." The students should have completed this assignment and have their papers ready. Have them exchange papers among themselves. Then, direct them to identify each of the three parts of the feedback model by underlining. If a part is missing, have them put a question mark. Remind them that the order of the parts may be mixed. Finally, have the students return the papers to their owners and then discuss any concerns or problems that resulted.

**III.** (5-10 minutes) Procede by turning to p. 90 and Activity 5.2, "Time for Another Compliment." Ask them to think of that person now. If someone is unsure and wants to use the group for some help, then work through the model with them. You might take the group members on an imaginative "walk through." Ask them to think of someone who has done something to make them have some positive feelings . Have them close their eyes, if it helps, and tell them to picture what the person has done (or does). This will help them to be more aware of the first part.

Now, ask what feelings come to mind as they think of what the person has done (or does). Is it pleasant or unpleasant? What are some words to describe the feeling. They can consult their feeling word lists later. Finally, ask what those feelings make them want to do or say. This mental practice is valuable preparation for giving feedback.

**IV.** (10-15 minutes) Conclude this session by reminding students that compliments are especially fun to give and receive. They can bring a little sunshine into the lives of people with the feedback model. Focus attention on compliments at this point. Confrontations can come later, after the students have more experience and confidence.

Finally, ask them some of the chapter review questions.

Assign pp. 91-101 *(BFH)*.

## Review Questions for Chapter V

1. What is feedback? What value is it?
2. What are the three parts of the feedback model?
3. What is the difference between a compliment and a confrontation?
4. When is it best to give compliments? What times are best to give confrontations?
5. What do people fear most about confrontations? About compliments?
6. Do people ever hear enough compliments? When was the last time you complimented someone?
7. Can you coach someone to give feedback to his or her friends, if the person doesn't know the model?

## Sessions Sixteen and Seventeen
## Looking at Yourself and Others

When students know themselves better, they learn more effectively and efficiently. Sessions Sixteen and Seventeen help students identify areas in which they feel confident and those that they want to improve upon. Increased self-understanding enables facilitators to have more insight to the problems of others and to be more patient with them.

## Chapter VI Highlights *(BFH)*

In this chapter students take a closer look at themselves and others by learning more about self-image. Four areas are recommended as a place to start in search of more self-understanding: *1) physical self; 2) beliefs and attitudes; 3) skills and abilities;* and, *4) self with others.* Exercises provide interesting information to students which encourage discovering and thinking.

**Guidelines for Training**

**Session Sixteen: Your Self-Image (pp. 91-101 *BFH*)**

The self-image is the focus of this session. "The self-image is the picture that you have of yourself and it affects the way you do things." Students also learn the effect that a negative self-image or a positive self-image might have on a person's actions.

Your training group has probably become more cohesive at this point. Exercises and practice with the helping skills have a way of fostering a togetherness. Self-disclosure and self-discovery to this point also bring the group closer in friendship. Thus, there is a readiness for more self-exploration and self-understanding through additional study of self and self-images.

This particular part of the training is an excellent opportunity to use training as treatment, especially if you have a *target student* in the group. A *target student is someone whom you have deliberately put in the group to give them some extra attention and help.* . Self-exploration and accepting responsibility for self seems more meaningful to these students when it is done as part of training or developmental learning, rather than through a confrontation with an authority figure during troubled times. Because target students are usually less defensive and feel support, these sessions can have a pronounced positive affect on them.

**I.** (10 minutes) Start the session by asking the students, "How much do you like yourself?" "How did you feel shaking your own hand? Did you do it? If not, what kept you from doing it?" "What difference does it make whether you like yourself or not?" "Can you like yourself too much?" "What are some examples of inner-talk that influence what you do?" Discuss the value of knowing more about one's self, as a part of helping others.

**II.** (10 minutes) Now, turn to pp. 93-94. "How did you feel about answering these questions?" "Which one was the most difficult? The easiest?" take time to discuss any of questions that the students want to share.

**III.** (5-15 minutes) Discuss the case of Sally (p. 95) and Jerome (p. 97). Then, the cases of Becky (pp. 99-101 and John (p. 101). Encourage the students to answer aloud the questions posed in the chapter.

— "How did Sally's thought affect her test results?"

— "Could she do better, if she saw herself positively?"

— "What did you learn about Jerome?"

— "How might Jerome's self-image affect his decisions?"

— "How did feedback affect Becky's behavior or actions?"

— "What did Becky have to be proud about?"

— "What part does size play in being popular with boys? Girls? Adults?"

— "What does it take before someone takes action to improve his or her physical self?"

In this session, physical-self receives special attention. Young students are going through important growth changes and some are becoming more aware of their bodies and appearances. Upper grade students are showing more marked differences. They may be a little self-conscious but it is an excellent opportunity to help them think about what they are experiencing in this growing and sometimes worrisome stage of life.

Help students explore how their attitudes about physical-self influence the activities they like, the way they enter a group or classroom, and how they participate in other areas of their lives. Help them become aware of their differences from primary grade students.

**IV.** (5-10 minutes) Conclude this session by asking the group members to write down two aspects of physical-self that they could improve upon. This is a private self-assessment.

Assign pp. 102-110, including Activity 6.1 (p. 108), "Looking At Your Self-Image."

## Session Seventeen: Looking at Yourself (pp. 102-110 *BFH*)

Session Seventeen continues with a focus upon self-image. Attention is given to the three other aspects of self: beliefs and attitudes, skills and abilities, and self with others. Students are encouraged to think about the cases provided in the chapter and to take the self-inventories (Activities 6.1 and 6.2).

**I.** (5 minutes) Begin the Session by discussion self-image. Beliefs and attitudes not only influence our behavior, but we encounter other beliefs and attitudes as we go through life. Sometimes our values are challenged. In the case of Juan (pp. 103-104) students think about how skills and abilities can influence self-confidence and interactions with others. Finally, the way we are with others can be influenced by how they respond to us.

**II.** (10-15 minutes) Talk with the students about Activity 6.1 (p. 108), "Looking at Your Self-Image." "How did you feel about doing this activity?" "What did you learn about yourself?" "Which question (or area) was most difficult to think about?" "How do you think your parents would fill out this inventory about you?" "What about your teachers?" "Your friends?"

**III.** (10-20 minutes) Proceed to Activity 6.2 (p. 110) "Incomplete Sentences." Pair the students and ask them, in turn, to share and discuss the first eight items. Then, call time and ask the students to be in another pair. Students then share their responses to the last eight items. Encourage the listener to be a facilitator as the partner talks about the experience.

**IV.** (5 minutes) Conclude this session by asking the chapter review questions.

Assign pp. 111-116, Chapter VII *(BFH)*.

**Review Questions for Chapter VI**

1. What is meant by the term self-image? How is it formed?
2. What are four self-image areas that you can use to help others think more about themselves?
3. What can people do if they don't like their physical self?
4. What determines whether a person is "skillful" or not?
5. What value is there in self-understanding? What part does it play in making decisions and solving problems? What part does it play in creating conflicts and problems?
6. What are some steps that a person can take to change a "self-image?"

## Session Eighteen
## Putting it All Together

This is a time for students to practice putting what they have learned into some meaningful pattern. At least one session will be needed for this experience.

## Chapter Highlights

There is no corresponding chapter for this session in the student book. In this meeting students are given an opportunity to put what they have learned into practice. Rather than role-play, students share something about themselves that they would like to change.

## Guidelines for Training

During this session, students will work in pairs and practice the helping skills that they have learned to this point: careful listening, the helping responses, the problem-solving model, and feedback.

**I.** (5 minutes) Begin this session by saying, "Today we are going to talk about ourselves. Each of us have something that we would like to change. Can you think of a change that you would like to make with yourself?" Give time for everyone to think of something. "Does everyone have something in mind? Okay, you are going to work with a facilitator and explore your ideas."

**II.** (20-30 minutes) Next, divide the class into pairs. All get equal time to share their "desired change." Facilitators take their partners through the problem-solving model, using all of the responses that they can. "You will have about 10-12 minutes each. I'll let you know how the time is going. Okay, begin now."

As the pairs are working together, move around the room and sit to the side of the pairs. Try to be unobtrusive, but make mental notes of how the students are working together. What kinds of responses are you hearing?

Keep accurate time so that each student gets an equal opportunity to be both a talker and a facilitator. At the end of the first round, call time. Even if they have not completed all steps, ask the facilitator to give the talkers some feedback, using the feedback model. Then, ask the partners to switch roles and start again.

At the end of the second round, call time. Ask the facilitators to give some feedback.

**III.** (5-10 minutes) Conclude this session by asking the students as a large group to discuss the experience.

Assign review pages relevant to the concerns and problems observed or expressed by students. Also, assign pp. 111-116, Chapter VII, *(BFH)*.

## Sessions Nineteen and Twenty
## Becoming a Friendly Helper

Students are now ready to complete the training sessions outlined in this book. They will also complete their readings in the student book. Although additional training sessions might have already been integrated or be planned for the future, these two sessions provide a closure to the core of the training program.

## Chapter VII Highlights

This is the final chapter in the student book. It provides a brief description of the four helping roles around which the program is designed: student assistant, tutor, special friend and small group leader. Questions that other facilitators have asked stimulate student thinking about concerns that they may have, as they prepare to help others. Finally, some supportive and reassuring statements from those who have worked with student facilitators are provided. There is also a certificate to be signed by the trainer when a student has satisfactorily completed the training sessions.

**Guidelines for Training**

**Session Nineteen: Four Roles and Some Helping Moments (pp. 111-116 *BFH*).**

This session gives attention to the four helping roles that are commonly found in a comprehensive student facilitator program. Facilitator projects and other student help can be defined around these roles. There will probably be some overlap in the roles and helping skills can be applied variously in all of them.

**I.** (5 minutes) Begin this session by asking, "What are the four helping roles for student facilitators?" Discuss the meaning of each role—its focus and general purpose.

It is probably timely to focus on anxiety students might be experiencing about working as facilitators. Discuss some of their concerns and questions. You might begin with a discussion of the sample questions that were of concern to other facilitators (pp. 115-115).

**II.** (20-30 minutes) Ask the students to think of their own concerns, perhaps some problem moments that they might encounter in their roles or projects. If it helps, ask each student to write down at least two questions that they would ask experienced facilitators from another school, if they could talk with them. Then, collect the papers and read aloud some of the concerns or questions. Discuss each one.

Be sure to respond to the feelings behind the questions or ask the group to identify the feelings in the questions. Next, elicit ideas or possible ways to answer the questions or work with the problem moments. Encourage the students to explore all their ideas, rejecting none. All are possibilities. You might role-play briefly a few responses. For example, "That sounds interesting and practical, but how would you say that?" or, "If you were in that situation, what would you say next?" And, "Where would you start?" "What responses would be most helpful at that time?"

Here are some situations that could be used for discussion purposes, some of which are likely to be brought up by students.

— What's a helpful opening statement to say when you first meet a "special friend" who is in the second grade?

— What should I do or say, if the person wants to keep talking, but I have to leave?

— What should I say when my friends ask me why I am talking with the little kids?

— How do you work with a person who doesn't want to talk or starts acting up?

— What if my special friend doesn't show up for our meeting?

— How do you set limits with someone who wants more time than you can give?

— What should I do if the person starts talking about something very personal and serious?

— What happens if a person starts to cry? To get mad? To run away? To get silent?

— What happens when the helping responses don't work?

— Should we tell a student what to do, if we have a good idea?

— What happens if my little friend won't talk with me? If he won't even look at me when we talk?

— What are we going to get out of this?

This is a time when students will look to you for answers. You are the expert in their eyes and most will believe that there is a correct response or answer to everything. Help them learn that this is not so. Let them explore alternatives. Ask them what they would do? What else could they do? You might use this opportunity to model the techniques of problem-solving (see Chapter V, *BFH*).

Many times anxiety will disappear or be reduced dramatically when students: 1) learn that they are not the only ones feeling anxious; )2 realize that others have faced similar problem moments; 3) discover some alternatives; and 4) get involved.

Sometimes, however, too much talking about potential problems only raises anxiety. It can create needless fear. Therefore, focus on the positive and be both reassuring and encouraging without dismissing student feelings.

It may be necessary to talk about ways to refer people to others who can provide more help. "What are some guidelines to use when encouraging persons to see someone else?"

You might:

1. Respond to their feelings and show some understanding.
2. Use the problem-solving steps.
3. Give them some positive feedback (a compliment about what they have done thus far).
4. Ask them who else they might talk with about their problem? Encourage them to see someone.
5. Ask if they would like to have you go with them.

**III.** (5-10 minutes) Conclude this session with a summary of the feelings that were expressed. ("What feelings do you hear in the session?") Emphasize that you will be continuing to explore their interests and concerns in the next session, as they begin to think of ways to be helpful. Ask them to start thinking of ways and places in which they can be "friendly helpers" in the four different roles.

Assign pp. 117-119. This is the final reading in the book.

### Session Twenty: Getting Ready to Help Others (pp. 117-119 BFH)

In this final session of the advanced training program, students discuss ways in which they can be of help around the school and other places. In addition, the students provide each other some positive comments (feedback) before being "officially" awarded the certificate of merit at the end of the book.

**I.** (10-15 minutes) Open the session by asking the students to name the four helping roles that were discussed in the previous session. Then, ask the group, "Given these roles and your helping skills, what are some ways in which you can individually or as a group help others—here at school, at home, or other places?" This is a "brain-storming" activity in which the ideas are listed on a large piece of paper (or chalk board) and discussed briefly. If time permits, students might express their personal preferences as a place to start. Or, the group might rank order the ideas for consideration in a future project.

**II.** (15 min.) *Strength Bombardment.* Have the students sit in a semicircle with one chair in front of the group. Then, each person in the group takes a turn, including the trainer, and sits in the chair. While in the chair, the person remains quiet while the rest of the group "bombards" that person with positive statements, compliments, or favorable remarks. Allow about one minute per person. There is no interaction or discussion until a person's turn is completed. Some students may want to use the feedback model, but this need not be required in order to speed up the process and to get everyone to participate. As trainer, be sure to comment once or twice to each person. For example, "I like your smile." Later, "You have a way of showing interest with your eyes that is really neat." Or, "You're a good sport."

*Strength Bombardment*, or variations of it, is designed to focus on student strengths. In the event that someone makes light of the task or says something negatively, simply interrupt and say, "Remember, we are focusing on the positive—tell what you like." Almost without fail, this experience is a very positive one that leaves students feeling special, important, and liked. The feedback model can always be used later to clarify or qualify statements.

*Awards!* Decide where and when the students will receive awards. Make this a special moment for them. The following are some ideas for presenting awards.

1. Students stand up individually. Praise their accomplishments as you give them an award.
2. Invite the principal, teachers, parents and/or other witnesses to the occasion.

3. Present the awards in an all-school assembly. Thus, other students might be motivated to meet with facilitators or to become facilitators themselves.
4. Present the awards at a school board meeting.
5. Take pictures of the "graduation ceremony."

**IV.** (5-15 minutes) Conclude the session with any appropriate remarks that will let the group know how important they have been to you and any positive feelings that you have as a result of working with them. Sign their certificates, if that is appropriate in your plans for them. Issue your congratulations to each one. Tell them when they will meet again—to prepare for projects. In the meantime, they can look for opportunities to put their helping skills to work—to be friendly helpers.

### Supplemental and Additional Sessions

The twenty training sessions provide the basic foundation for a training program. The supplemental activities that follow (see Appendix) can be used for additional training or experiences. These might be integrated into the training sessions described in this chapter, inserted as additional training sessions, or used as needed with supervision and follow-up.

Chapter VII of this book provides some evaluation measures that could also be used as part of training. For example, pre- and post-tests might be used to start and end the training program. They might also be used to assess a particular project or a certain skill.

Some additional sessions would, of course, be appropriate at the end of the tenth session, if students are to engage in some beginning projects. Likewise, additional sessions might be needed if some immediate projects are undertaken at the end of the fifteenth session. Finally, after all training is completed, there will be a need for meetings to plan and supervise follow up on projects. The nature of projects, and the supervision of them are the subject of the next chapter.

# Chapter VI
# Implementing and Supervising Projects

>   Step 1: Making A Commitment
>   Step 2: Forming a Plan
>   Step 3: Enlisting Support
>   Step 4: Selecting Student Facilitators
>   Step 5: Training the Facilitators
>
> **Step 6: Implementing and Supervising Projects**

Now that the students have completed some initial training, it is time to put their new skills and knowledge to work in some school projects. Though facilitators might spontaneously be helpful as occasions arise, organized projects based around the four helping roles provide a more specific vehicle where students and faculty can work together. Projects help maximize the impact of the program. They enable a trainer or coordinator to talk more specifically about what students are doing and accomplishing. They also give the program more visibility and credibility.

*Projects are "field experiences" with planned procedures. They have defined roles, objectives, plans of action, and provisions for supervision and assessment. They are usually designed for a particular group or population. They are often planned in sequential steps, taking student skills into consideration. Most have a time-line around which events or activities are scheduled.*

There are many different kinds of projects. Some are determined by the levels of student skills, while others are devised because of special needs, interests, or opportunities. In some cases, projects evolve because of particular faculty memebers who are interested, imaginative and supportive.

## Implementing Helping Projects

As you start to think about projects consider the following: program level, who will be involved, objectives or goals, help that is needed from others, the facilitator roles or tasks, relevant activities, and organizational procedures. Plans that are carefully constructed tend to inspire student (and trainer) confidence, elicit more administrative and teacher support, and generally are more successful.

**What is the Program Level?**

All projects might be viewed in terms of three levels: beginning, intermediate or advanced. The level of a project is commensurate with the helping skills and self-confidence that students have obtained, as well as their training phase. Some projects are planned deliberately to provide practice with certain helping skills. Some focus upon specific roles or special tasks. Others are even more comprehensive in scope. They may require more specific preparation and planning.

**Beginning Programs and Projects.** A beginning student facilitator program is more than just a starting place. It is characterized by the skills that are taught, the length of the training schedule, and the projects that follow. In a beginning program students are introduced to a few fundamental concepts. These include: 1) the characteristics of a helping person and a helping relationship; 2) the importance of being a careful listener; and, 3) how to ask relevant questions, clarify ideas, and respond to feelings. Other concepts and skills may be just as important in a helping process, but these three are singled out for attention in a beginning program.

With limited skills, the facilitators will not be able to fill all the roles that are part of a comprehensive program. Projects are more limited in scope and time. There is closer supervision of activities and these are more tightly organized. There is more structure. Because the facilitators are less experienced, they usually perform fewer tasks in a project.

**Intermediate Programs and Projects.** An intermediate program is characterized by the addition of more helping skills and extended projects. For example, in addition to the concepts and skills learned in the beginning program, decision-making and problem-solving, as well as feedback, are added. These additional skills allow the facilitators to be involved in a larger range of projects. For instance, feedback enables them to give and facilitate compliments among students.

Confrontations and the setting of limits are also possible. A problem-solving model helps students make decisions and, consequently, facilitators work more confidently with those who are experiencing problems in school.

Intermediate projects are a natural extension of beginning ones, although there is probably less need for structure and more time is alloted for interactions. Facilitators assume more responsibility and supervision is not as close. Nevertheless, special attention is given to reviewing the basic skills and mastering new ones.

**Advanced Programs and Projects.** Advanced programs are the goal of most coordinators and trainers. They are the most comprehensive because facilitators have progressively assumed more responsibility and work in more varied roles. By this time, facilitators are familar with the helping process. They know the basic communication skills and have had some supervised experiences. Facilitators in an advanced program tend to have more self-confidence and are ready for more challenges.

Because the trainer has closely supervised the early stages of development, there is probably less need for close supervision in some projects. Rather, more attention is given to problem moments. While there are still some structured activities, advanced facilitators are capable of initiating the helping process without detailed procedures. Their judgment has usually been tested and refined. They know themselves better and they are more aware of their limitations.

Because of the extended scope of the program and projects, they also know how to refer students who need more help than they can give. They are encouraged to be more spontaneous in their work and to seize upon opportunities in their daily lives to be friendly helpers. There is more self-exploration at this point too, as they encounter more difficult situations and recognize the contributions that they can make to others. The steady progression of students is important. Little people take little steps, but they eventually get where they are going. They don't need to be dragged along by a strong-willed adult who urges them to hurry up. Have you ever seen a mother or father who was unaware or indifferent to the small steps a child takes? These parents seemingly take giant steps. The child is moving little legs twice as fast as the adult. Such a pace is bound to be confusing, fatiguing, and a bit frightening.

Effective trainers slow the pace. They are patient. With careful planning and supervision, facilitators will move successfully and progressively from beginning to advanced programs and projects.

## Who is Involved in Projects?

There is usually a specific population of students or target group for each project. In one project, for example, fifth grade facilitators worked with small groups of second grade students during a social studies unit. In another case, some facilitators worked individually with a few fourth grade students who were identified as shy and not participating in class discussion.

The students with whom the facilitators work might be chosen by the trainer and teachers. Or, the facilitators themselves might participate in the decision. One girl in training especially wanted to work with first grade girls, if given the opportunity. A boy in the same training program expressed an interest to be involved in a project with fifth grade boys who were trying to organize a basketball team. Sometimes facilitators develop their own individual projects in cooperation with a trainer. On other occasions the facilitators and trainer work together to plan a group project.

In situations where "training is treatment" the roles and projects are especially selected so that the experience is mutually beneficial to the facilitator and student who is receiving help. For example, Cal was a facilitator who had been identified by his teachers as disruptive in class and a troublemaker around school. He told the trainer that his teachers were mean and didn't like him.

As Cal moved through the training session, he learned to communicate more effectively with others and to have more personal control of himself. After his advanced training was complete, he met with a fourth grade teacher during recess and talked with her about some disruptive students in her class. They explored the problem and some ways to resolve it. As a consequence, Cal became more sensitive and responsive to his own teacher. He was friendlier and more responsible, although he still managed to "get into trouble" on occasion. Nevertheless, there was some marked improvement in his behavior around school.

Do you want your trainees to work with individuals or groups? What grade level do you have in mind? What groups or populations are available?

## Who's Help is Needed?

Teachers and parents can be valuable resources. They can help you think of projects. Some may be of direct assistance in particular projects. As they work with you, they also learn more about your program and can become part of your support base.

In the case of Cal, the fourth grade teacher volunteered to talk with him about a problem that she was having with some of her students. She was asked not to role-play but to explore a real concern, as Cal led her through a problem-solving model. It was to be a spontaneous sharing and exploring time for her. While Cal was to be the primary benefactor, in that it gave him an opportunity to practice his helping skills, the teacher also benefited. She had a chance to think through some ideas about the situation.

In another project, a trainer enlisted the help of some parent volunteers to sit in on a small group meeting with facilitators as they led a discussion about "the generation gap." The primary objective for each facilitator was to make at least three helping responses to comments expressed by the parents.

Without faculty support, projects will be limited. Even with their interest, however, be considerate and thorough in how you "contract" with them for projects. Teacher permission for student participation in training and helping projects is a primary consideration for the trainer.

## What are the Objectives of the Project?

Begin by identifying what you hope the facilitators will accomplish. Think of specific goals and objectives for the project. Make a list. Review and prioritize the items on it.

Avoid a pitfall that trips some trainers: too many goals and expectations in a single project. One project can build upon another. Linked together, several projects can lead toward an ultimate goal. Other gains may occur along the way.

One project involved a second grade classroom, where students met with facilitators in small groups. Each student was to be given an opportunity to say something about friendship, to be responded to by a facilitator and to relate at least two ways in which students can be better friends. Facilitators followed a structured outline for some group activities. The objectives were clearly identified.

## ...ies, Tasks and Skills are Needed?

...ective set of proceedings and procedures in ...s take part. There is usually an organization to ...akes the experience interesting, meaningful ... They are often designed to help participants ex- ...concept, gain insight, and move toward some goal.

...ple, the supplementary activities in this book might be des... bed as learning experiences. Though some might view them as games, they have specific directions and expectations. In almost every case, these activities will further personalize the learning experience.

Tasks within activities are leader behaviors (e.g. questions, directions, comments) that keep the activity moving in a desired direction. Sometimes they come at planned stages or phases of an activity. At other times they occur when the participants do something to elicit the "next task." A facilitator must understand the essential tasks of any activity before initiating it. On occasion, especially with beginning projects, facilitators may need to have a sequential list of the tasks, either in mind or close by, for reference.

In addition, facilitators can use the "helping skills" to enhance the interaction during a task. Sometimes it is possible to anticipate the helping skills that will be needed or directly related to a particular task in an activity. Facilitators might practice these skills and be ready to use them.

Your projects will be organized around certain activities, tasks and skills. Which ones will the facilitators need and use? What experience do they have with them? Are the tasks structured appropriately to their skill level?

## What Are the Organizational Procedures?

There are a few items that might be on your checklist for projects. Among these are some organization procedures:

**Place.** Where will the project and related activities take place? What minimal space is needed? Are moveable chairs available or will students sit on a carpeted area? Are there electrical outlets for facilitators who want to tape record the sessions? What distractions can you anticipate as a result of where you are meeting? How much privacy can you expect? What will you need to tell the facilitators about the use of the place where they will be working?

**Time.** How long will a session within a project take place? That is, will facilitators meet with a group of students for 15 or 20 minutes? Will facilitators who meet individually with younger students work with them for 10 minutes or for as much time as they can on a certain day? What times are facilitators available and how much time is used moving to and from a project area? How much time is needed to start, to carry-out a task, and to conclude?

**Duration.** How long can a project reasonably last? Some projects have a series of events, each leading to a subsequent task or event. These are sometimes planned in advance. At others times, they develop as a consequence of the question, "If the facilitators continued to meet with the students in your class, what would be the next goal or experience?" Some projects are limited to one or two meetings. Others are designed for ten or more. Negotiations with teachers and administrators may be necessary for scheduling student itme.

In general, plan a project for a certain duration that includes an expected number of helping events or sessions. Then, after these sessions are completed, you can contract again for some more sessions. It seems advisable to leave a situation where people are asking for more help from the facilitators than being trapped in a long and tedious project that must be cancelled or revised. When projects are of short and specific duration (one grading period, two weeks, ten sessions, etc.), then you will feel in control of the project, have fewer interruptions, and stay on schedule.

**Assigning Facilitators to Students.** How will facilitators initiate their contacts and make arrangements? Will you pair students and facilitators based upon your knowledge of a situation, and perhaps with the help from a teacher? Or, will you let the pairings occur randomly? Will you draw upon teacher referrals? Does the situation call for co-leaders or will one facilitator lead the group? How many students and facilitators will be involved in a project?

If you have five facilitators, for example, who are planning to work with some first grade students, the facilitators might first visit the classroom and observe. Then, after some discussion among themselves, they might identify the students who they believe would best work with them.

**Activities.** Will a project have specified activities? Which ones? How are they related to facilitator skills? Are any of the activities more appropriate for some grade levels than others? Can they be adapted to individual, as well as group sessions? How are the activities related to one another? Do they line up in a meaningful series? What tasks are essential and which ones are desirable? Do the facilitators understand how to start, proceed with, and conclude the activities they will use?

**Materials Needed.** Some projects require the use of paper or art materials. Others need kits or posters. What materials will students need in their work? Where will you get them? What plans do you have to ensure that the materials are available when needed, returned after use, and used properly? For example to do a pencil-paper activity with a special friend as a means of helping that person think through the situation. The materials needed must be available.

There are probably other items that might be added to your checklist. With experience you will learn which ones are the most critical. In addition, as others in the school come to know about the program, experience it, and support it, then some considerations will no longer take on the same significance as they did when you first started.

As you think about the four helping roles, you might identify many projects in which student facilitators can take part. The list is limitless. What follows are some ideas that you might draw upon.

## Student Assistant Projects

This time-honored role is expanded upon through a student facilitator program. Projects that involve student assistants are often determined by the school's curricula, policies, and special activities. Many times, opportunities are lodged in historical or traditional events associated with the school or community. There is a difference among schools regarding seasonal events and programs. These programs could be enhanced through more student involvement. The imagination and willingness of faculty and administration obviously affect projects that involve student assistants.

### Counselor/Teacher Assistants.

There are some routine tasks associated with teaching and counseling where students can be of assistance. Some of these are rather menial and may not involve much student interaction (e.g. grading papers, preparing materials for a class lesson, constructing a bulletin board, taking messages to the office, passing out workbooks, and helping take attendance). Likewise, counselors might use a guidance assistant in the office to help prepare activities for group guidance sessions or work with some minor clerical duties.

In a beginning project, for example, one school established a station in the hallway which was made primarily of cardboard. Drawing upon the Peanuts cartoon characters, a large sign read: "The Counselor is In" (or out, as the case may be). Student facilitators were assigned to be in the booth before school, during lunch, and immediately after school. Any student could approach the person in the booth and ask a question about the school, activities for that day, or how to see the real counselor. Students could sign up for special school events, receive messages, and offer suggestions which were passed on to the counselor and principal.

Facilitators were encouraged to use some helping responses with each student who approached the booth. For some beginning facilitators the tasks were: First, clarify student comments before responding to their request. Respond to their feelings. Think of some other ways in which you might be a friendly helper to students who stop by the booth.

In intermediate and advanced projects, facilitators could spend more time with those who stop by the booth. Some interview appointments could help students further explore their concerns or ideas and suggestions. In one school, facilitators announced that they would be available at the booth to listen to suggestions about the use of equipment or the cafeteria area. Some of these encounters lead to some "special friend" projects, where more extended interaction and help took place.

Other ways to assist teachers and counselors might be: work on the playground as an assistant to the teacher who is on duty; help with younger students at a bus stop;help kindergarten students get ready to catch a bus; escort students to the cafeteria, or to the gym for a film or special program.

Counselor assistants might be on duty in the guidance office and greet students when the counselor is busy. They can take messages and help students think of a time when they could meet with the counselor. Some might help recruit students for a small group guidance activity. Others might work as social reinforcers, confederates, or models.

**Orientation.**

Providing an orientation experience for new students is an important guidance activity. New students are often in need of help. They may be unsure of the school facilities, policies and procedures, or opportunities. Some may be scared or confused because of the strange surroundings. A friendly person can help orient them to their new environment and make them feel important. A facilitator can make a difference in how a young child, who is new to a school, responds when parents ask that first evening: "Well, how do you like your new school?" Or, "How did it go today?"

In a beginning project, facilitators might be given the task of talking with a new student and then following an interview outline. The outline might contain some questions, perhaps two or three tasks. "What was your last school like?" "How do you feel about moving to this school?" "How's it going so far?" To each of the responses, the facilitator would be encouraged to listen carefully and make either a feeling-focused or clarifying response.

More advanced students might develop their own outlines, conduct a more in-depth interview, and use more helping skills. In addition, they might be given the task of following-up with the student for a given period of time (e.g. two weeks). They could answer more questions and help the new student talk more about the experience of attending a new school.

In an advanced project, for example, facilitators can also prepare students for a different school or program. For example, a group of sixth grade middle school student facilitators traveled with their counselor to a nearby elementary school for an orientation program with fifth grade students. The counselor talked with the large group about routine matters and gave them an official greeting. Then, the group was divided into smaller groups for 15-minute discussions. Student facilitators acted as group leaders.

The facilitators prepared for this project by discussing some anticipated questions and concerns. They also recalled their own experience of moving from the elementary school to the middle school. They had a set of questions that could help stimulate discussion, if students were reticient. For example, "How do you feel about going to the middle school?" "What is one thing that you have heard about the middle school that you like?" "That you are unsure about?" "What do you think it will be like?" "How do you think it will be different?"

Each facilitator was directed to first respond to student feelings—to draw the feelings out before answering quesitons or making suggestions. In one situation, two facilitators co-led a group, with one acting as a recorder of questions. These were later turned over to the counselor, who attempted to answer some of them in the large group. During the small group experience the counselor and fifth grade teachers moved among the groups and gave personal attention to some.

This experience also enabled the younger students to have a "contact person" or special friend at the middle school. It personalized the orientation. It emphasized that middle school can be a positive experience. The message: "We care about what you are feeling and thinking at this time. We want to be of help. We are friendly at the middle school."

**Greeters and Meeters.**

This term was used to describe a role that some middle school student facilitators assumed when visitors came to their school. The "greeters" wore badges that identified them as student facilitators. They handed the visitor written material about the school (e.g. map, roster or teachers, classroom schedules, and school calendar). They were coached in how to greet visitors, to make them feel welcome, and to take them on a tour of the school, if requested. Visitors, including parents in the community, are usually impressed when students lead the tour and point out different things, even though a counselor or principal may "tag along" with the group.

The facilitators might also provide this kind of help at a Parent's Night, when many more visitors are in the school. The approach provides a more personalized experience for parents. It emphasizes that the school is child-centered. Students get an opportunity to interact with adults in a mature and responsible way.

**Enhancing School Morale.**

Morale is a powerful force, for better or for worse. It can either drag a group down or give it energy. For example, when the hostages in Iran were released and returned to the United States, citizens rallied around the event and experienced a common loyalty. There was a common purpose that inspired people, brought them together, and made them feel proud to be citizens of the country again.

Likewise, a school can become more exciting and productive by building student enthusiasm and morale. This is often evident when students rally around a team as it prepares for competition. Team spirit has a positive effect on the school's learning climate. There is pride in the school and in student accomplishments.

Facilitators can help improve school spirit. For example, they can use the feedback model to compliment students in the school. Students can take more pride in others' successes as well as their own. In a beginning project, asistants might organize a fun activity such as a "Guess Who Contest." This game features baby pictures of students or faculty. The "Cutest Feet" or "Helping Hands" contest is also a starting place for student interest and involvement.

A school newspaper or quarterly newsletter also offers possibilities. Facilitators might help identify winners of a "Peace Prize" given to a student once a month who helps the school be a better place in which to learn.

In an advanced project, assistants might organize a "School Spirit Club." With volunteers from different grade levels, the club could develop projects which promote more school loyalty and cohesiveness. The focus is on the positive, in that students are friendly and care about each other. For instance, the club might hold a pep rally, as was done in one school, prior to the administration of some school-wide assessment tests. Other rallies might focus upon achievements of students and give them some deserved recognition for being a positive part of the school.

Poems or songs might be written which would focus on school morale or effective school behaviors. One group composed rhymes for children to use while jumping rope. The words emphasized the importance of working together cooperatively.

**Other Student Assistant Projects.**

The following are some more ideas for projects in which students can apply their helping skills. Each might be organized along the lines of a beginning or a more advanced experience.

— Safety patrol members can use helping responses while assisting students to and from school. In an advanced project, they might work with their advisor to organize a safety program for different classes, perhaps putting on demonstrations, panel discussions, or brief presentations.

— Student council members might use the responses in their meetings. More advanced training would enable them to be better leaders by meeting with their "constituents" in group discussions. The problem-solving model might be used to help students work through a general problem that is facing the student body (e.g. racial integration, school morale, vandalism, or a traumatic event that has caused general concern in the school).

- Student assistants at a Parent Teacher Association or Organization meeting—perhaps as greeters and meeters.
- Student members on a school advisory board or community board.
- Educational media center specialist, assisting with equipment and presentations.
- Library assistants, perhaps providing a reading circle experience for young children. Or, helping in a book search service.
- A school nurse assistant, to talk with students who are not feeling well before or after they meet with the nurse.
- Phone message takers.

## Tutor Projects

When student facilitators work as tutors, their primary attention is directed to helping students in an academic subject area. Tutoring might be done individually or in groups. However, it could focus on attitudes as well as skills and concepts.

The traditional tutor tends to focus upon subject matter almost exclusively, giving little time or attention to the learner. Facilitators use communication skills to help students explore their ideas and feelings in the learning process. They also model or demonstrate skills and teach concepts. Drill and repeated practice can be a part of any tutoring experience, but facilitators will also take time to focus on the learner's experience, special needs, and interests.

Facilitators support, reinforce, confront, and encourage students in their school work. They can also make tutoring fun. What was once a tedious learning task can be more enjoyable.

Cross-age tutoring is very popular in schools because it gives tutors an opportunity to apply their skills. Subsequently, the skills become reinforced in the tutors. Here are some tutoring projects for student facilitators.

### Language Experiences

A language experience program is one way of personalizing learning. A child learns that: 1) What I can think about, I can talk about; 2) What I can say can be written by me or by someone else; 3) What I can write, I can read; and 4) I can read what other people have written for me because they use most of the same words I use when I talk and write. Thus, the child's own language is the basis for dictating or writing self-developed materials.

In a beginning project, facilitators might copy what young students say (a few sentences) and help them read what was copied. Or, facilitators can be careful listeners and tape record a story that a student has told. Asking open ended questions about the story and clarifying the responses will help the students become more familiar with language and story telling techniques.

In an intermediate project, facilitators who have more skills might structure a situation that encourages students to make up a story. Using the problem-solving model, facilitators could help students to explore possible solutions. Facilitators might be instructed to look for at least one opportunity to give some positive feedback and use the feedback model in giving a compliment.

In an advanced project, a facilitator might meet with a group of students who are reading something that they wrote. The facilitator, as group leader, can encourage the group members to talk about their experience. Pictures, for example, might be drawn to illustrate parts of stories. The facilitator asks questions, clarifies ideas, and responds to feelings. Thus, students experience an atmosphere of positive sharing and acceptance. Everyone's work is acknowledged and the facilitator provides an opportunity for a child to communicate thoughts, to learn that one's contributions are valued and respected, and to obtain some positive recognition from others.

More specialized tutoring with a particular skill or concept will depend, of course, upon the skill of the tutor. However, given the context of such a positive and personalized learning process, facilitators will feel more comfortable in pointing to ways in which a paper might be improved technically (e.g. spelling, punctuation, capitalization).

Academic skills can also be incorporated into a social topic that deals with friendship, classroom behaviors, or sibling relationships. Such a project would allow more one-to-one attention and might be useful for helping students who have not been participating in classroom activities and who perhaps need more encouragment than a teacher has time to give. It is also valuable for low-ability students who must work hard to compete and gain recognition for their efforts. It is especially helpful with culturally different students who have difficulty in communicating.

## Learning Centers

The learning center is a popular approach to individualized learning. It is an area in a classroom which contains a collection of activities and materials that help students learn, clarify, or practice a skill or concept. They can be used to reinforce a teacher-taught lesson, although sometimes they are comprehensive enough to replace a regular lesson. Individuals and small groups of students may work at the centers at various times during the day.

The success of a learning center will depend upon the materials, the organizational pattern of the classroom, and a teacher's guidelines and personal commitment. However, with the help of student facilitators, even on occasion, success is much more likely. There is more room to be creative in developing centers that involve student interaction. With the help of charts, bulletin boards, teacher guides, evaluation instruments, and their own personal resources as facilitators, "friendly helpers" can teach their classmates and personalize the learning process.

Let's look at an example. A friendly helper could be stationed at a learning center in math. At that station students might study measurement concepts and practice related skills. They could learn to use different measuring devices and about fractional parts. They could also develop their estimation skills. Several games and activities might be available (e.g. Kaplan et al., 1973).

From a "build it box" children could measure pieces of pre-cut wood and follow directions on a card that instructs them how to build a simple object (e.g. boat, car, house, etc.). In another box there might be a variety of measuring tools. Children could measure different objects and record their data on a chart. In a third box, a pair of dice is used and one is covered with fractions.

Children take turns throwing the dice and then cut a narrow strip of paper to show the length in inches as shown on the dice. The first student to make a single line that totals 20 inches is the winner. Or, objects of different lengths might be in another box. Children could estimate how long an object is and then measure it, recording their estimations and measurements before consulting an answer book.

Other tasks might also be included at the center (e.g. Find out how many teaspoons are in a cup; measure four parts of your body and list them in order from shortest to longest; measure something around (circumference) and up and down (height); make a display (montage) of measuring devices; drop different items and use a timer to compare how fast they fall; collect things that weigh between one and two dekagrams.

Facilitators who complete the beginning phase of training might be instructed to pose some questions to students about each task, both factual and personal in order to help them think about the learning experience. They could follow a leader's guide and perhaps clarify a student response and then respond to at least one feeling that they noticed among students who participated in the center. Simple listening tasks might be outlined so that they could give some focus to a brief discussion with a student.

Facilitators who have completed the intermediate phases of the training program might be more involved in leading students in discussion. They could apply the problem-solving model, as students learn the lesson. They might also make it a point to give students positive feedback about the way in which they took part in the task. Discussion questions might be provided by the teacher, or students could develop their own questions and have them approved by the teacher.

Advanced student facilitators with more experience might play an even more prominent role in facilitating students to think about their lessons and experiences at the center. For instance, they might work with a small group at the center and lead them in a discussion about what they learned and experienced, including their own attitudes and behaviors as they approached the tasks.

They might also develop their own learning center or tasks for centers that would enable them to encourage students. Target students, those needing special attention and encouragment, might be identified so that the facilitators could be more supportive and reinforce their efforts when they arrive at the center.

## Study Circles

A facilitator could lead students in some exercises in a study circle. Teachers frequently find it helpful to divide their classes into small homogeneous groups. It enables them to provide for individual differences and needs, as well as for more student interaction and involvement. For instance, it's possible for a teacher to have one group of students at a learning center, a second group in the library doing independent study, another group in a study circle with a student facilitator, while giving individual attention to a final group.

If assigned to a reading circle, a student facilitator might read aloud (or listen) to students. A discussion related to the reading might follow. Or, students could meet in a writing circle to share their assignments, perhaps reading and correcting them together. Sometimes the study circle is used primarily to motivate students and clarify assignments.

A beginning student facilitator could meet with a small group of students in a circle, showing them some pictures which go with a story that is being played on a tape recorder. After the story, the group could ask four questions that have been planned as follow-up. The facilitator's task might be to have each student in the group comment at least once.

More advanced facilitators can lead students through extended activities and expanded discussions. For example, a facilitator might follow-up a story by asking students to think about a time when they experienced something similar in their own lives. First, they talk about it. Then, they write about it. This kind of writing circle can motivate students. It helps them organize thoughts, identify feelings and clarify important ideas. As students read their written statements later, the facilitators could ask the group members to summarize ideas and to identify feelings. Depending upon the skill of the facilitator(s), more technical aspects of the writing might also receive attention.

Several study circles or discussion groups might take place at the same time. On one occasion, a teacher read a short story to the class. To provide more opportunities for student interaction and disscussion, student facilitators were assigned to each of five small groups composed of about 5-6 students. The task for each facilitator was to lead the group in a discussion about the story and to elicit a comment from each member of the group.

Finally, the facilitator gave some positive feedback to the group about their behavior and ideas, telling some feelings that were experienced while working with the group.

## "Catch-Up" Helpers

Student tutors can also help other students who have missed a lot of school because of illness During their extended absences these students tend to get behind in their classwork. They may return to school feeling confused, anxious, and fear that they will never catch-up. Teachers give as much time as they can to helping these students make up their work, but they rarely have enough time to do what they would like to do. This concerns them. They worry that these students might get even farther behind because they lack some fundamentals that are related to current lessons.

Facilitators at all levels can be friendly helpers and provide some timely assistance to those who need to catch up. In addition to reviewing assignments, giving some suggestion and directions, facilitators can listen to a student's concerns. Beginning facilitators will probably concentrate on helping students catch up in their assignments and responding to feelings of anxiety, pressure, and so on. More advanced students, on the other hand, can use more skills to help students resolve problems that are associated with their extended absences. They can help them assess their circumstances and provide some timely support.

"Catch-up" projects might also be appropriate for new students who have transferred to the school and who are now behind in their work. Or, perhaps a new student did not receive certain kinds of instruction at the other school which is pertinent to new assignments.

Catch-up is not necessarily working with a slow or handicapped learner, but this is also a possibility. In this case, the project might be re-defined and goals more clearly deliniated.

## Skill-Building Demonstrations

Sometimes facilitators can work closely with a teacher as part of a skill-building demonstration. In this case, the facilitator plays a role in a presentation and demonstrates a particular skill. For example, if the skill is to operate a machine in a science project, the student could model the skills as the teacher talks about the principles behind the apparatus. The facilitator could then answer questions and perhaps coach other students.

These ideas are only representative of what student facilitators might do as tutors. With appropriate instruction, they can serve as models, reinforcers, discussion leaders, monitors, and teacher assistants. The way in which they interact with other students in tutor roles can make a difference in how they are received and the kind of impact they have. Training student facilitators assures teachers and counselors of having more skilled tutors, ones who are not only academically able but who are sensitive to what a learner is experiencing. This increased sensitivity and the communication skills that go with being "friendly helpers" enable them to really facilitate the learning process and provide a positive experience for tutees.

### Special Friend Projects

There are many students in school who would like an opportunity to meet with a student facilitator and talk about themselves and their ideas. They like to share their thoughts and discover more about themselves and others. When students are excited about something, they want to talk about it. They want to be with someone who will listen to their enthusiasm and share their experience.

There are, of course, some students who need more personal attention because they are feeling alienated from school, teachers or parents. These students worry about some of the events in their lives. For example, if a young student is having a difficult time at home or school, that student may feel lonely, isolated or rejected. Withdrawl or agressive behavior may be an out-let for the frustrations that may be building. When these students have a "special friend" who listens and encourages them to get the most out of school, then there is more positive growth. Some frustrated students act out their unpleasant feelings in a way that is disruptive to their own and others' learning. These students can make school an unpleasant experience for everyone. Yet, with timely help and assistance, they might be able to talk out their feelings and find more meaning in school.

Student facilitators can provide timely support and encouragement by being a "special friend." Special friends take time to listen, to show interest in what a "friend" is experiencing. They help friends to explore problems, to think of alternatives and to take positive actions. Friendly helpers tell their friends that they are important.

**Big Brothers and Sisters**

Little children frequently look up to older siblings and their friends. Too often, however, members in the same family are so busy with their own home and school experiences that they fail to help each other. Sometimes family expectations get in the way and children may fear that their feelings may not be accepted. Some children have no real brothers or sisters with whom to talk.

For these and other reasons, the idea of big brothers and sisters has been a popular one. Upper grade students might be assigned (or choose) "a little buddy." Times are then made available for them to talk and work together.

The buddy system has often been related to tutoring. But, it may also evolve into a "special friendship." Special friends explore many ideas. There are fewer restraints or directions. Young students can choose to use the time in anyway that they want—to get some tutoring, to play a game, to talk about an idea, to explore a problem. As little children experience the helping conditions and learn that their special friends will listen, they turn to them in time of need. Ideally, however, friendships and helping relationships develop prior to a problem or crisis. They emerge out of positive times together.

Big brothers and sisters can provide a link for some students that leads to more involvement in school. On occasion, typical problems that confront young students are discussed (e.g. kids picking on them, name calling, fear of failing, hating tests, worried that the teacher doesn't like them, or being bored and uninterested in school).

Sometimes big brothers and sisters can work closely with teachers, perhaps directing special talks toward a particular topic or concern of the teacher. At other times, they might be a "social reinforcer." Being with an older buddy for a play experience might be one rewarding contignecy that could motivate a student to complete assignments or make adjustments in class.

**Secret Pen Pals**

Facilitators might also be secret pen pals to younger students. They could be assigned to observe students in a class or on the playground. Then, when appropriate, they might write their "special friends" brief notes and comments about something positive that they learned or noticed about their behavior.

For example, "Today I learned that you completed all the questions in your reading assignment. Congratulations!" Then, it is signed, "Your Secret Pal" and a smiley face is drawn underneath it. At another time a note might read "Hi! You got a higher grade on your paper yesterday! That's neat!" Or, "Sorry to hear you were sick. It made me feel sad. Hope you catch-up with your school work soon." Or, "You have a nice smile and it makes others smile back. I'm impressed."

As suspense builds, the teacher and secret pen pal can arrange a time for a meeting of the two "friends." Then, they can talk about the experience. Young children are almost certain to be flattered that someone is noticing positive things about them. Some ideas, of course, can be provided to a pen pal by the teacher. This can be a novel and fun experience. It sometimes introduces friends who become supportive of each other for a long time.

**Pairing for Friendship**

Students can choose, or be assigned, a buddy with whom to study for a grading period. Times could be set aside so that the pairs review assignments together, work on a study unit as a team, and prepare for tests together. A few teams of equal or close ability might compete with each other in an assignment.

For example, two students might add their scores together and compete against the added scores of another team. This experience might lead to more opportunities to talk about school and their classwork. This in turn might build more trust and caring, which would lay the groundwork for times when a "buddy" wants to talk about a problem or concern. One of the team members could be a facilitator and the other a "target student."

**Other Special Friend Projects**

- Place a sign up list on the guidance office where students can indicate an interest in talking with an older student about a problem.

- Announce a topical project (e.g. astronomy; motor bikes; back packing) in which students can sign up and talk with a special friend about the topic.

- Have facilitators identify someone whom they would like to get to know better. They initiate a conversation with that person and try to find out at least three new things about that person.

- Start a study group, then introduce a more guidance centered topic that the group could discuss (e.g. "What makes people happy? How can people work more cooperatively together? What do you like best and least about school? What's one thing that would make school a better place for you?"

- When a foreign student arrives at school—encourage the students to teach and learn from each other.

Members of the students' families also need special friends. Facilitators might be encouraged to think of times when each of their family members could use their help as special friends.

As the program progresses, students will find more opportunities to spontaneously help others, some of which may develop into special friendships.

The young man who attempted to assassinate President Reagan was a distraught person. He had few friends. He was a loner, as were so many other assassins. Would he have benefited from having peers who cared? Could he have talked with a facilitator about his concerns or problems? Would such an experience have reduced his alienated feelings and prevented a tragic event? Might things have been different if he had been a target student in a facilitator program?

A student facilitator program helps a school become a more friendly place. It creates more chances for friendships to develop, even though some become closer than others.

Projects are designed to foster friendly relationships. They encourage students to "reach-out" and be a positive part in someone else's life. In the process, they also provide more opportunities for students to use their helping concepts and skills. Interestingly enough, when a "special friend" initiates a friendship, that person often gets back more than just a chance to practice helping skills. When it comes time for the facilitator to look for a special friend, that friend may not be far away.

Facilitators themselves will have some ideas about being a special friend to others. Some will not like the idea of being a friend to someone who others tease or reject. It takes courage to reach-out in these cases. In addition, some will worry that being a special friend means that they must be friends at all times and do many things together. This need not be the case.

Knowing how to set limits on friendships may be worth discussing. Being a special friend does not mean that facilitators must enter a binding relationship. It means, however, that when they are with the person they act in friendly and helpful ways.

## Small Group Leader Projects

Students learn from each other through group experiences. This is especially true when group conditions encourage participants to share and explore ideas together. Unfortunately, groups in many schools are too large, too confining and restricted. Many students still sit in long rows and listen to teachers present ideas from the front of the class. Although this might be desireable, at times, rows are not conducive to stimulating class discussions. Limited eye contact, for one thing, discourages participation and group cohesiveness.

Competent counselors and teachers are aware of this serious drawback about large classroom groups. They try to find ways to put students into more appropriate groupings. They plan for times when a class can be divided into smaller discussion groups, where students can interact and become more involved.

Student facilitators can provide an excellent resource as small group leaders. Because they are knowledgable of the helping relationship and communication skills, they can create positive learning conditions and experiences in a group.

## Preparing for Small Group Experiences

The helping skills are usually taught to students as if they were going to work with someone on an individual basis. They are easier to practice in a one-to-one situation. There are fewer interactions than in a group. With an individual the facilitator has more control over the flow of the conversation.

Students usually learn about the helping skills, however, by being members of a group—a training group. Some of the group activities that a trainer uses are subsequently available for use with other students. Students can think of ways to apply the same activities in their own small groups.

In addition to the helping skills learned earlier, some additional preparation may be needed for times when facilitators work with small groups. In general, *it is best if the facilitators have experienced the group activity that they are going to use, either in training or a part of some specific preparation for a project.*

Facilitators might help design a series of small group experiences for a particular population (e.g. 4th grade classes) and then *"walk-through" the activities in an abbreviated experience before using them with others.* In this case, particular attention is given to 1) groundrules; 2) topics for discussion; and 3) helping responses in a group. Other things may also need attention, but they can be dealt with as the facilitators experience them.

**Groundrules.** Groundrules for a group are usually established in the beginning, although some may be added later if the situation calls for it. Generally speaking, student facilitators need a simple set of groundrules for leading groups. Groundrules help keep the group on task, make it more manageable and productive.

You might begin by asking the facilitators, "Can you think of some groundrules that will help students in your group work together?" "What groundrules in our own group have been helpful?" "Should groundrules differ from one group to another (e.g. first grade to sixth grade)?"

Here are a few groundrules that have been used by other facilitators with small groups:

1. Look at the person who is talking.
2. Everyone gets a turn to talk.
3. Listen so that you can tell what somebody else said.

For primary grade children, it may be necessary to add such groundrules as: raise your hand to show you want to talk; only one person talks at a time; stay in your seat until the group has finished; and, keep your hands to yourself.

Groundrules can be drawn from other sources (e.g. DUSO, Magic Circle, TAD, and others). However, some of these are too long and wordy, too negative, or unnecessary. On the other hand, some students already have some experience with them in their classrooms and they could easily be adapted. For example:

— "Stick to the point." (DUSO)

— "Don't clam up." (DUSO)

— "Raise your hand." (TAD)

— "You can pass." (Magic Circle)

— "Stay in your place." (Magic Circle)

— "Don't gossip." (Magic Circle)

Too many rules make the atmosphere oppressive, rigid, and threatening. Without any groundrules, a group may flounder and lack organization. Suggest that your facilitators start with a few groundrules. They might begin with the three most important ones to them—stated in the positive—and then add others if necessary.

**Topics.** What kind of discussions will take place in a small group? A lot will depend upon the communication skills of the leader and the focus the group gives to a topic. Almost any topic can be approached from an intellectual or personal point of view, or both. Here are some topics that students have found interesting:

— "The three best ways to improve grades"

— "How to get along with adults"

— "One of my favorite wishes"

— "One word I'd like people to say about me"

— "How our class can help conserve more energy"

— "A place the class could visit for a field trip"

— "Changes I would make in the cafeteria"

— "A famous person whom I'd like to have visit our school"

There are many interesting topics. Some are more interesting than others, but all can help students share their personal opinions and explore their ideas.

When topics are planned for a series of small group experiences, student facilitators can help think of those that are easiest to discuss in the beginning and those that lead to more self-disclosure and feedback as the group moves along. A series of discussion topics might be related to some general areas of interest or concern (e.g. helping at school; home; getting along with others; making decisions; study habits; planning for Valentines' Day).

Implementing and Supervising Projects

**The Helping Responses.** Ask the facilitators, "Which of the helping responses can be used with a group?" "How will it be different from using them with an individual?" Then, you might select a topic for discussion, either from a student list or one of your own choosing. Pose the topic to the facilitator group. Ask each member to think of at least one open question that could be asked about the topic and write it down on a piece of paper.

Next, read one of the questions and let someone in the group respond. Model a set of responses for the group (e.g. open question, clarify the response that you get, ask another open question of the group, then respond with either a clairfying or feeling response).

Show the facilitators how such *a set of responses* might be developed by them, as a structure to draw upon when working with groups. Other sequences might be developed.

**Published Group Programs**

During the 1970s several affective education programs were developed to assist children in learning more about themselves and others. Some were more systematic, organized and emphasized a curriculum approach (e.g. *DUSO,* 1970 and 1973; *HDP,* 1974; *TAD,* 1974). They provide sequentially planned activities and focus upon areas of self-development.

These published materials and others are excellent resources that can be used in guidance programs at all levels in the elementary school. Most important, many of them can be adapted so that student facilitators could provide the leadership to help students experience the activities and to discover their meaning. Let's examine some of these in more detail.

Developing Understanding of Self and Others (DUSO) is a guidance program that was developed by Don Dinkmeyer. *DUSO Kit D-1* (1970) is designed for use in the primary grades while *DUSO Kit D-2* (1973) is used with students at the intermediate grade levels. A variety of activities, posters, stories, songs, cassette tape recordings, puppets, and readings help children learn more about themselves and others.

In a beginning project, facilitators might work with small groups of first grade students, seating them in a circle. After playing a tape recorded story or reading it aloud, a facilitator can lead group members in a follow-up discussion. Inexperienced facilitators could follow the recommended discussion questions for each story, while incorporating the helping skills learned in the initial phases of their training. Intermediate and advanced facilitators might use the role-playing cards and supplemental activities that go with each lesson.

A beginning facilitator might contract to meet with a small group of five second grade students, either in or out of the classroom. The first four *DUSO* stories are interesting and could be an appropriate place to start. They focus upon groundrules and help students learn to work together.

More advanced facilitators might lead the group through several lessons and perhaps use more supplemental activities. They might also work with a "target group." With the help of the trainer and teacher, they could select some stories from *DUSO* that would be particularly relevant. Or, a story might be selected because of a "target student" who is in a group. With planning, students can explore behaviors, values, and experiences that are directly related to a need or concern of the group.

*The Human Development Program (HDP)* is often referred to by its popular name of "Magic Circle." Harold Bessell, Ulvado Palomares and Gerladine Ball contributed to it. It is an organized "share and tell" experience where students sit in a circle and discuss given topics. Discussion tasks are sequentially arranged and related to social and emotional development, self-understanding, self-confidence, and human relations. Each session usually lasts between 10 and 15 minutes.

During Magic Circle, students take turns going around the circle and responding briefly to such tasks as: Think of a time you did something but wish you hadn't; Tell about a time when you felt proud; Tell about something you wanted to do but didn't. In most instances, students share their thoughts briefly and little attempt is made to help them elaborate upon their responses.

The Magic Circle format was used by one group of third grade facilitators in a 1st grade project. The facilitator first worked with the school counselor and experienced several sessions of the Magic Circle. They later practiced acknowledging contributions and clarifying responses. Two of the experiences which they enjoyed and seemed interesting were selected. They then led groups of first grade students, with about four to the group, through the same experiences. The counselor sat outside the group to supervise and offer timely coaching.

*Toward Affective Development (TAD)* was developed by Henry Dupont, Sue Gardner and David Brody (1974) for use with children in grades three through six. Again, the approach is a curricular one, with 191 classroom lessons built around 21 guidance units. Student facilitators, however, might examine the kit and then select some of the activities for use. Like *DUSO, TAD* kits have useful materials, including cassette tapes, discussion pictures, games, and supplemental activities.

## Structured Group Experiences

There are many structured group activities scattered through out the professional literature. Many of them were developed and became popular during the 1960s when the "growth group movement" received so much attention. Others were developed during the 1970s when the emphasis was upon self-help, communication skills, and values clarification. In particular, Pfeiffer and Jones (1975) collected numerous group activities and published them in several volumes.

Simon, Howe, and Kirchenbaum (1972) described several values clarification activities. Some of these are appropriate for training facilitators and can subsequently be used with groups of students. Canfield and Wells (1979) published a book which described 100 activities that could be used to improve self-concept in the classroom. These activities could be adapted for use with and by facilitators.

Some published activities are more effective at eliciting certain group dynamics and discussions than others. Some need to be used by a skilled counselor, or not at all. Others require little expertise and can lead to a valuable experience with minimum leadership. It is adviseable to develop a series of activities that follow a logical sequence and that are pertinent to the goals and objectives of your program. This might be done with as few as two students, or as many as time allows.

Feelings classes were first introduced by Verne Faust (1968). He believed that children needed to learn more about feelings and to understand how feelings are related to behaviors. Further, he advocated that such instruction be incorporated into the regular school curriculum, about twenty minutes a day, since it was so directly related to learning efficiency and effectiveness.

Wittmer and Myrick (1980) later expanded upon the concept and described more than 80 activities that might be used in feelings classes. The major objectives of a feelings class are:

1. *To help students become aware that feelings exist.* This involves a sensitizing experience for them. Only after they are sensitized to feelings can they learn to effectively deal with them.

2. *To help students become aware that all feelings are experienced by all people.* That is, students need to learn that they have many feelings in common with other students and that they are not alone in their experiences. Learning that others also feel the same way, at times, tends to reduce feelings of inadequacy and guilt, which so often causes excessive anxiety and ineffective learning.

3. *To help students learn that one need not act out every feeling.* All of us learn to inhibit certain behaviors or channel certain feelings in socially effective ways. There is no need to ignore or to deny feelings, even those that are labeled in our culture as undesireable. Ignoring or denying feelings creates defensiveness and distortion that leads to ineffective thinking and behavior patterns.

4. *To help students learn socially effective ways of expressing feelings.* Some behaviors are unacceptable to society. Helping students to identtify feelings and channel them into socially effective behaviors is an essential aspect of all learning.

These objectives might be realized through almost any group procedure, providing that they are given attention and remain a primary focus of the group experience.

## Discussion Groups

Structured group experiences are an organized effort to use special activities and specific group tasks. The activities are usually designed to elicit ideas, behaviors, or special experiences. However, it is also possible for facilitators to lead small group discussions that are relatively unstructured.

During "group sessions" students share ideas about a general topic. Since there are no special activities or tasks, the group facilitator must rely upon the helping skills to focus or shape the discussion as it unfolds. Perhaps the group may struggle to brainstorm ideas about something. In another situation, the group might react to an experience. The facilitator responds to each group member with open questions, clarifying and feeling responses, while encouraging other group members to do the same. At the end, the group might summarize some of the ideas or conclude by sharing a final feeling or thought about the group discussion.

On occasion, a teacher might want a student facilitator to lead a small group discussion in the classroom. The topic could be related specifically to a class lesson. For example, a small group might discuss the meaning of a story that was read in class. Or, group members might discuss the review questions that are posed at the end of an assigned reading. Sometimes a set of questions provided by the teacher can guide the group discussion.

## "My Friends and Me" — A Beginning Project

One small group project that might be used with students who are in the beginning stage of training is a guidance unit entitled "My Friends and Me." This project previously referred to as the "Gainesville Project," emphasizes the successive approximation of leader behaviors in a group.

Facilitators are given a set of structured group experiences with carefully designed tasks. These tasks keep the group moving and centered on the topic.

   **I. Description of the Project.** This project is designed for primary grade children (second graders) to participate in some small group discussions led by upper grade (fourth or fifth graders) student facilitators. There are four sessions in which a second grade class is randomly subdivided into five or six small circle groups, each led by a trained facilitator. The focus of the circle group discussions is friendship and peer relations.

   **II. Objectives**

   A. Objectives for the student facilitators:

   1. To be a small group leader and lead participants through selected tasks—related to friendship.

   2. To practice helping responses in the group — acknowledging each participant, responding to feelings, clarifying ideas, and asking open questions.

   3. To set the tone of the group by modeling facilitative skills and caring behaviors.

   4. To outline the groundrules for the group and to help personalize the experience through the use of names and other encouraging behaviors.

   B. Objectives for the group participants:

   1. To learn more about themselves and others through various tasks related to the topic of friendship.

   2. To have an opportunity to listen to others and to practice listening skills.

3. To have an opportunity to speak and be heard.
4. To have an opportunity to self-disclose ideas about peer relations and to experience an accepting, understanding, and caring relationship.

## III. The Small Group Procedures

A. The counselor and teacher can consult with each other to determine the assignment of facilitators and students to groups. Generally, this is done at random.

B. It might be helpful to have name tags for the first group session.

C. Circle groups should be arranged without tables. Open space is better because physical obstacles can be barriers to communication.

D. The counselor and teacher will "supervise" movement of students to the circles and, on occasion, sit in or near a group if it seems advisable. However, once the groups have been situated, the facilitators should be responsible for leading the task and making the responses. Later the facilitators meet as a group and discuss the experience. One of the major objectives is to keep the experience positive, which supercedes any task or leader behavior.

D. The teacher and counselor can be the time-keepers and give signals as time draws to a close. If some groups take longer than others, the counselor or teacher might join those groups for any further discussion. If some facilitators can continue leading—let them lead.

## IV. The Small Group Tasks and Sessions

A. **Group tasks.** Group tasks are topic statements. The facilitator gives the statement and, in a go-around participants respond. Each session has at least two related tasks. All tasks are related to the general theme of friendship and peer relations. The specific tasks for this project are identified below in each of the group sessions.

B. **The Small Group Sessions.** There will be four 15-20 minute sessions. Groups meet once or twice a week. The facilitator leads each session and is responsible for implementing leader behaviors—facilitative responses—as suggested below.

C. **The Group Leaders Role.** The small group leader or facilitator reads or give each "task" in order. Suggested responses follow the task, thus providing some structure and focus to the member's participation. Another example of group problem-solving is *Cooperative Helping*. A few students sit together in a close circle.

**Session One: "Getting Started."**

Task 1: Introduction of participants. In a "go-around," students introduce themselves. If name tags are not available or used, the "name-game" might be played as a second way of learning names.

Task 2: The facilitator tells the members what the group will do in their meetings—focusing on learning about self and others through talks about friendship.

Task 3: The facilitator introduces the basic ground rules for the group:

1. Look at the person who is talking.
2. Listen for the person's feelings, as well as ideas.
3. Relax and be patient.
4. Tell the person or group what you heard.

Task 4: The facilitator says, "Tell about a time when you did something with a friend."

Facilitators can: a) reflect feelings, b) clarify statements, and c) acknowledge contributions (e.g. "Thank you" or "Thank you for sharing that"). Nothing more is expected or required.

Supplementary Task: "Who can remember what someone else in the group said?"

**Session Two: "What's In a Friend?"**

Task 1: The facilitator says, "Who can remember our group's groundrules?"

Facilitators clarify the groundrules.

Task 2: "Today we are going to name some things that you look for in a friend. Let's go around and each person name something."

Facilitators use the same three leader responses from response.

After each member's contribution, the facilitator now asks one open ended question, listens, acknowledges and moves around the group as before. Thus, the person is encouraged to speak twice—once to the task and then to the open question.

Task 3: "Now, tell something about yourself that you think will make you a good friend."

Facilitators continue with same leader responses as before. If time is limited, the number of open-ended questions might be reduced or eliminated.

Supplementary Task: "Who can remember what someone else said in the group?"

**Session Three: "What Do Friends Share?"**

Task 1: "Who can remember our group's groundrules?"

Facilitators help review the groundrules.

Task 2: "If you could give something to a friend to make that person happier, what would it be? Let's go around and each person name something."

Facilitators use, perhaps mixing the order, the leader behaviors of:

1. reflecting feelings
2. clarifying statements
3. acknowledging
4. asking one open-ended question

Move around the group as before and respond twice to each person.

Task 3: "If someone could give you something to make you happier, what would it be?"

Facilitators continue with the same leader responses as before. If time is limited, the open-ended questions might be reduced or eliminated.

Supplementary Tasks: "Who can remember what someone else said in the group?" "How were some of the answers the same or different?"

**Session Four: "Making Friends and Learning About Others"**

Task 1: " Who can remember the groundrules?"

Task 2: "Tell one way that a person can make new friends."

Facilitators use leader skills as they wish or as they seem appropriate: reflecting feelings, clarifying statements, asking open-ended questions, and acknowledging. This may be an open discussion rather than a go-around if desired.

Task 3: "Tell us something you learned about someone in this group from our sessions.

Task 4: Tell what you liked or didn't like about our group.

After completing this beginning project, facilitators should have more self-confidence as small group leaders and be ready to move on to advanced training and projects.

## Problem-Solving Groups — Advanced Projects

More advanced facilitators can help a group to resolve problems. For example, they might be particularly helpful with a small group of students who are part of *in-house suspension*. One or two facilitators might help suspended students to explore their difficulties and to think about some responsible alternatives.

The facilitators will, of course, avoid statements like "You should. . . ," or, "You shouldn't have. . . ." Using their skills, facilitators can help make the suspension more meaningful than if the students are just left alone to "think about what they have done."

Another example of group problem-solving is *Cooperative Helping.* Some students sit together in a close circle. Other students form a larger circle around them. One student in the center volunteers a problem or concern to discuss, while one or more facilitators help bring it into focus. Next, the center group members offer suggestions. These are recorded by two students in the outside circle, who take turns writing the ideas. Suggestions are not evaluated as good or bad.

Later, students in the outer circle add ideas to the lists. Facilitators then add their suggestions. Finally, the lists are collected and given to the volunteer who keeps them and decides privately which ideas to consider. If time allows, inner and outer circles change places and the process begins again with another volunteer and new recorders.

As an alternative, facilitators might devise a story about a student who is faced with a dilemma (e.g. being offered drugs, being asked to shoplift, being pressured to fight someone or tell a lie). One facilitator might role-play the problem moment. The students in the center circle explore what might be done in the situation. Then, outside circle members can volunteer to exchange places with someone in the center group to share ideas. Facilitators could also follow the five steps of the problem-solving model.

Implementing and Supervising Projects

## Facilitators as Co-leaders

Some trainers prefer that facilitators work with students as co-leaders, especially in the beginning. However, this can add to confusion, unless the facilitators have some ideas about their respective roles. For example, one might open the discussion, while the other listens for feelings expressed and responds to them. Or, one person might lead the group through the first part of an activity while the other leads during the second part. In another instance, one might model behaviors for the group while the other focuses upon the tasks.

If the group activity is complicated or more difficult, then co-leaders can support each other and provide a source of checks and balances. When the group is relatively unstructured, co-leaders can work togehter to give the group focus and follow the leads given by the group. However, the ultimate goal is to help each facilitator feel confident in leading a small group discussion by oneself.

## Supervision

Student facilitators are not school counselors or teachers. They are not certified professionals with a record of competencies. They are not employees of the school system and have no contractual obligations. They are unpaid for their efforts. While some might receive special recognition and attention, most rely upon the intrinsic satisfaction of knowing that they have been a friendly helper to others and that they have done the best that they can. The realization of their impact upon others and their potential as a valuable resource in a school can only be achieved through careful supervision.

Supervision is not something to take for granted. It can not be regarded as something which is available to students if needed. Rather, supervision is an essential component of a comprehensive student facilitator program and is a scheduled part of all projects. During supervision student facilitators discuss their helping experiences. They need and want an opportunity to talk about their work, including their joys and frustrations. Give them a chance to talk openly about their concerns. Encourage them to explore what they have done and what they might do. It can be a valuable learning experience as they examine their behaviors, their feelings, and the facilitative skills they used in a situation.

When you provide supervision, student facilitators continue to grow and develop their skills. They feel more supported and less alone, especially as they listen to other students talk about their most and least successful moments. From supervision they gain a sense of direction and feel motivated to continue in their efforts. It is a renewing experience, one that keeps the energy level high and the enthusiasm strong.

And, there are still other advantages:

— Supervision leads to a higher quality program. More difficult tasks can be undertaken by facilitators who receive guidance and support.

— Supervision builds self-confidence in both students and coordinators. There is greater awareness of what is happening, of the progress that is being made, and of the next steps that need to be taken.

— Supervision provides the trainers and coordinators with feedback so that additional training might be planned, if appropriate. Additional projects result from student progress. Future training programs can be revised based upon the information received in supervisory meetings.

— Supervision enables the coordinator to speak more confidently about the program, its accomplishments and the direction it is taking.

— Supervision provides some reassurance to administrators and teachers who want the program to be successful but who may be skeptical about student abilities.

— Supervision provides timely assistance to facilitators and their helpees when problems develop beyond which a student facilitator might feel competent.

— Supervision gives support to certain facilitators who depend upon or need more guidance or direction.

— Supervision provides opportunities for the program to be individualized for the facilitators and their project interests.

— Supervision offers interesting learning experiences for the facilitators.

— Supervision prepares some facilitators for more advanced experiences and projects, including target groups and students.

Student facilitators will apply their helping skills in many situations. Some will be more spontaneous. Somethings happen at home, in school, or other places where the facilitator can use the skills learned in the program. Even these occasions can sometimes lead to a supervisory session with the trainer or coordinator.

John was a student facilitator who came upon a situation in which two of his friends started arguing. Each accused the other of "cheating" in order to win a game. The more they talked, the more angry they became. Tempers flared and a fist fight resulted. A teacher stopped the fight and warned them about the consequences if it occured again.

Subsequently, the two boys would not speak to one another and avoided being in the same vicinity. John spoke with his supervisor about the situation and explored his own feelings and behavior when the fight occured. He said he felt helpless and did nothing to stop it, except to say, "Hey, you guys are going to get in trouble. Why don't you forget it and let's get on with the game?" He thought about some other things he might have said. More important to John, however, was finding some next steps which might help the boys become friends again.

In other situations, supervision will be closely tied to a helping project. It might even be arranged at a certain time when the facilitators meet individually or as a group to discuss their experiences. The complexity and length of a project may determine how much supervision is needed and when it would be most appropriate. When it is delayed for too long a period of time, it becomes more difficult to provide guidance and direction. Moreover, the facilitator without supervision can become frustrated, discouraged, and lose enthusiasm.

**Supervision Methods**

There are several procedures that you might use to supervise students. First, both individual and group supervision should be available. Some facilitators may be too embarrassed to talk in front of a group about a particular situation they experienced. Others might worry about violating a helpee's confidence, especially if the situation is a sensitive one that needs to be treated privately. On the other hand, group meetings can reduce your own time commitment, add to the group's cohesiveness, and help students learn from each other.

Supervision is the process of exploring a helping experience with the facilitator involved. It is usually after the experience has taken place and when the student has time to think about the situation. However, it might also occur on-site, such as in a classroom during a small group project.

Direct observation of students helping others in a project has many advantages. The supervisor can observe the process and take note of behaviors and dynamics that are occuring. The supervisor might even intervene if the facilitator needs timely assistance or coaching.

For example you might:

— Be present in the classroom when the facilitators are working with small groups. Move around the room and listen for the tasks and helping statements in an unobtrusive way.

— Sit on the edge of a group, making no attempt to participate or intervene. Take mental notes of the situation.

— Observe students through a one-way glass or window, if it is available. Or, use a video tape recorder to observe while in another room.

In many cases the supervisor will be one step removed from a facilitator's work and will need to rely upon supplementary reports. In this case you might:

— Use audio tapes or video tapes to observe students in action. Have the students record a few minutes of a group or individual helping session.

— Collect some self-reports from the helpees who are working with the facilitators—perhaps a checklist or Likert-type scale (Strongly Agree to Strongly Disagree) could be used.

— Ask teachers for their observations and ideas.

— Encourage co-leaders to report what they experienced, inviting them to give each other feedback.

— Use role-playing to re-enact a situation so that the group might provide some reactions and suggestions.

— Arrange a meeting during lunch when facilitators can share their experiences.

Encourage, or require, facilitators to keep a diary or log of their experiences. They could record their feelings, as well as what happened. Caution them about the confidentiality of their logs (e.g. avoid writing names or specifics about the person and focus on the helping process.)

**Supervison Strategies**

Supervision can be a very personal experience for the supervisor and the facilitator. Because facilitators are sharing their work, there is likely to be some anxiety, threat, and fear of being evaluated. Most facilitators by this time will be anxious to do well and to please the trainer.

If students do not experience the "helping conditions" in supervision, they will not be as open or interested. There will be more defensiveness and an excellent learning opportunity could be lost.

Here are a few guidelines that you may want to keep in mind as you supervise your facilitators:

1. Give astudent a chance to talk first. How did it go? What did you do that you liked? What would you change? How do you think the helpee would have described the experience? What are your plans now?

2. Model careful listening and the helping responses during supervision.

3. Use the feedback and problem-solving models.

4. Help the students to identify their strengths, as well as what they might improve upon. Tell them what you saw or heard—without judging. Get their reactions.

5. When a student is struggling to improve and things are not going well, help the facilitator concentrate or practice one or two things.

6. Set limits when necessary. Give specific directions if appropriate. Beginning facilitators especially need more structure and support.

7. Timely reassurance is usually helpful at the end of a session.

8. Inspire confidence through a positive and encouraging attitude.

9. Be sensitive to times when individual supervision is more appropriate than group supervision.

Student facilitator programs must provide some form of supervision. Without it a program could become unmanageable, lack direction and risk loosing support. Learning opportunities for students and trainers would be lost. With carefully planned supervision, however, a program can become more comprehensive and facilitators can experience more success in many different kinds of helping projects.

# Chapter VII
# Assessing and Evaluating Progress

> Step 1: Making a Commitment
> Step 2: Forming a Plan
> Step 3: Enlisting Support
> Step 4: Selecting Student Facilitators
> Step 5: Training the Facilitators
> Step 6: Implementing and Supervising Projects
>
> **Step 7: Assessing and Evaluating Progress**

Are the facilitators ready to help others? Is the training program working? Are the facilitators benefiting? What has the program accomplished? What are your future plans for the program?

These and other questions will be posed to you. They may be asked at different times from many people. They might be asked in other ways and in some unusual places, but people will want to know more about your program and its effectiveness. Some questions and answers effect especially the development, perhaps survival, of your program. For example, "Is the program making a difference?"

Assessing and Evaluating Progress 217

## Why Assess and Evaluate?

New ideas are introduced to schools every year. Although changes may seem slow and tedious to some educators, they are inevitable. Some changes are dramatic and uproot traditions. Others evolve slowly from old ideas that have been modified slightly from time to time. Some last for a long time, while others disappear rapidly.

Educational change or permanency results because ideas are evaluated. Ideas are dropped or revised, and new ones are substituted or added, all depending upon the judgment of someone.

The purpose of assessing student progress is to collect information which might be useful in making decisions. Periodically evaluating outcomes is a professional activity which is part of the trainer and coordinator's role. If you fail to do so, then others will do it for you. Or, decisions could be made with insufficient and inappropriate data.

If you want to have continued support and to receive deserved credit, assessment and evaluation should not be left to chance. Rather, an organized approach should be included in your plans.

## Sources of Information and Evaluation

There are different ways to make assessments and to collect information. At least four common sources of information might be considered: 1) outside experts; 2) standardized tests; 3) behavioral referrants; and 4) self-reports.

**Outside Experts.** The development of student facilitator programs is relatively new. There are very few, if any, who would claim the title of "expert." However, there are many people who have studied or helped develop programs. These "experts" might be from the county or district staff, a university or college, a community agency, or perhaps an established program in another school system. They qualify as "experts" and consultants because they have some knowledge and understanding of student or peer facilitator activities and programs.

When outside experts or consultants are used to evaluate a program, it is common to collect some information and to let them examine it. If there has been a systematic effort to collect valid data, then the information will have more meaning. In addition, the experts might talk with people who are involved in the program, observe some training activities and watch some facilitators in action. They could also administer a questionnaire to collect their own data.

Unless there is a given set of criteria to judge a program, outside experts must rely upon their own biases or understanding of what a program should look like and what it should be accomplishing. Therefore, provide them with a description of your program, it's objectives, and any other evidence that you think is relevant. You may want to develop a checklist which could guide them in making their assessment.

**Standardized Tests.** Published tests and inventories are available for measuring educational outcomes. Some will be more relevant to your program and the facilitators' work than others. There are, for example, standardized tests for intelligence, aptitudes, attitudes, achievement, and self-concept. Some of the facilitators' work may have a direct impact upon standardized test scores.

For instance, a group of second grade students may improve their reading scores as a consequence of working with facilitators who 1) help tutor them individually and 2) lead them through some activities in a study circle. A reading readiness or achievement test could help evaluate some of their efforts.

Yet, there are very few standardized tests that are specifically designed to measure all the objectives of a student facilitator program. It is often difficult to find ones that focus on a particular unit of work (e.g. tutoring in reading). Ready-made tests, if available, may not be as effective as coordinator-made instruments even though they may have the benefit of being standardized.

Building your own measuring instruments can also help you and your students define objectives. This often makes a measure more relevant than any external test is likely to be. Moreover, developing an appropriate measurement device also makes the process an integral part of the program and projects.

**Self-reports.** Asking people to report their own behavior referents, thoughts or feelings has long been a major technique of assessment. Subjective reports currently supply much of the information available regarding student effectiveness, achievement and attitude.

Some people regard self-reports as too unreliable and question their validity. They are also criticized as subject to influence by social conventions or a desire to please others. Yet, if they are accurate and honest, it is difficult to imagine a more dependable source of information. Self-reports are frequently used because they are easy to construct and administer.

Common sense will decide the kind of measures and sources of information you want to use. You may not have the time or resources to develop a comprehensive evaluation based upon a rigorous research design. The use of control and experimental groups can be appealing, but it is not a general custom of most schools. It can be time consuming. The lack of a research design or using one with limitations should not deter you, however, from collecting evidence about the outcomes of the program.

## Four Areas of Assessment

There are at least four areas of assessment that most trainers and coordinators are concerned about. These include: 1) development of one's self growth and improvement; 2) the acquisition of facilitator skills and concepts; 3) facilitator effectiveness with others; and, 4) the general effectiveness of the program. What follows are some sample instruments and measurement devices for these areas. They are meant to be illustrative and can be modified to suit your purposes. Or, other instruments might be developed that are more specifically related to program and project objectives.

### Self-Development

A focus on self-development might begin with the facilitators themselves. How much have they learned from the training sessions? How have trainers, projects or the program in general affected their personal development, communication skills and general attitude about others? Has it affected their behaviors in class, around school or at home?

**Attitudes Toward Others.** The *Attitudes Toward Others Survey* (Figure 7.1) is a brief measure of how students feel about others. There are twenty items to which a respondent can express agreement or disagreement. The items can provide some insight as to a person's degree of interest and anxiety when around others. Other items might be added. The survey might also be read to students.

## Figure 7.1
## Attitudes Toward Others Survey

**Directions**: Read each sentence. Circle SA, A, U, D, or SD for each item to show if you Strongly Agree, Agree, are Unsure, Disagree, or Strongly Disagree.

| | |
|---|---|
| SA A U D SD | 1. I am more comfortable by myself than with others. |
| SA A U D SD | 2. I don't like to be around young children. |
| SA A U D SD | 3. I am uncomfortable talking with people about their problems. |
| SA A U D SD | 4. It's okay for other students to believe differently than me. |
| SA A U D SD | 5. I am uncomfortable talking with a student who is a different race than me. |
| SA A U D SD | 6. I would rather not be around students who may need help. |
| SA A U D SD | 7. I have difficulty talking with most adults. |
| SA A U D SD | 8. Some people are born bad. |
| SA A U D SD | 9. All people have problems of some kind. |
| SA A U D SD | 10. I don't like students who have problems with school. |
| SA A U D SD | 11. I don't like students who are different from me. |
| SA A U D SD | 12. I become nervous when I'm around students I don't know. |
| SA A U D SD | 13. There are more people that I don't like than there are people that I like. |

SA A U D SD   14. I like the students in my school.

SA A U D SD   15. Students who talk about their problems make me uneasy.

SA A U D SD   16. I like to meet new people.

SA A U D SD   17. I don't really care about what others think and feel about things.

SA A U D SD   18. I am uncomfortable talking with girls.

SA A U D SD   19. I could be friends with a student who could not see—someone who is blind.

SA A U D SD   20. I am uncomfortable talking with boys.

**Assertiveness.** The *Assertiveness Assessment Scale* (Figure 7.2) is one example of a personality variable related to self-development which might be improved upon in a student facilitator program. Since the program focuses upon effective communication and leadership skills, it is expected that some students will show gains in their social abilities or self-confidence with others. Students learn to assert themselves in positive and sensitive ways.

The rating scale in Figure 7.2, developed by Meg Rashbaum-Selig and Anne Lally (1975), is an unpublished inventory for assertiveness training with young people. It was designed for use with students in a middle or junior high school. While some of the items might be eliminated or modified, the instrument attempts to provide some assessment of the degree to which students would assert themselves in certain situations. It is also possible that the items could be responded to through a Likert-type scale (Strongly Agree to Strongly Disagree).

**Figure 7.2**

**Assertiveness Assessment Scale**

**Directions:** Below is a list of actions. Rate yourself on each one. Mark your answers this way:

Mark 1 if you would *never* be able to do this action.
Mark 2 if you would *seldom* be able to do it.
Mark 3 if you would *sometimes* be able to do it.
Mark 4 if you would *always* be able to do it.

1 2 3 4   1. I can speak up in large groups when I have something to say.

1 2 3 4   2. I can speak up in small groups when I have something to say.

1 2 3 4   3. If someone interrupts me, I can stop that person and keep talking.

1 2 3 4   4. I can tell someone if I am annoyed with something that person is doing.

1 2 3 4   5. If a friend asks me for candy, and I want it, I am afraid to say no.

1 2 3 4   6. If a friend wants to copy off my paper, and I don't want my friend to do it, I can say "no."

1 2 3 4   7. If I have a criticism of someone, I am not afraid to tell that person face to face.

1 2 3 4   8. If someone teases me, I can tell that person how I feel.

1 2 3 4   9. If a teacher does something I don't think is fair, I can tell the teacher my feelings.

1 2 3 4   10. If my mom does something I don't think is fair, I can tell her.

1 2 3 4   11. If my dad does something I don't think is fair, I can tell him

1 2 3 4   12. If my friend asks me to do something that I think is wrong, I can say "no."

Assessing and Evaluating Progress

1 2 3 4    13. If my friend asks me to do something that I think is wrong, I am not afraid to tell my friend how I feel.

1 2 3 4    14. If my friend does something well, I can give my friend a compliment.

My goal: I would like to get better at _____.

**Attitude Toward School.** It seems evident that attitudes can make a difference in whether one is successful or not. For example, students who have a positive attitude about school seem to achieve more, have better interpersonal relationships with peers and teachers, and make more contributions to the school environment. Some counseling programs are directed to improving attitudes toward school, with the assumption that students will learn more and find more meaning in school. Teachers and principals recognize the importance of school morale and sense when students are developing a "negative attitude" about school.

A school attitude inventory can reflect a student's perception of school. For example, the *School Attitude Test* (McCallon, 1973) is composed of 46 items. It has some high reliability data and is published in both English and Spanish. A statement is given and students are asked to respond by indicating whether or not it is true of them "most of the time," "some of the time," or "not very often." For example, here are some items from the test that might be effected through a student facilitator program:

— I like my school friends.
— All the people at my school are friendly.
— When I need help everybody in school helps me.
— The people in my school like each other.
— The people in my school work together.
— The children in my school are good to me.
— The people in my school listen to me.
— I like my school.
— Going to school is fun.

These items, along with others, might be used to construct your own inventory, perhaps using a similar response scale or another of your choosing.

**Behavior Checklist.** Sometimes it can be helpful if students, teachers or counselors examine a checklist of behaviors and apply it to an individual. A student can be rated according to each item that appears on the list. Items can be substituted or added. They can be reworded to suit the situation, but must be written in observable terms. For example, the *Student Behavior Inventory* (Figure 7.3) may be used to help assess a student's achieving or non-achieving behaviors.

**Figure 7.3**

**Student Behavior Inventory**

**(Achieving or Non-Achieving Behaviors)**

**Directions:** Below is a list of behaviors. Rate the student's frequency for each one.

Mark 1 if you would *never* be able to do this action.
Mark 2 if you would *seldom* be able to do it.
Mark 3 if you would *sometimes* be able to do it.
Mark 4 if you would *always* be able to do it.

1 2 3 4 5   1. Completes work on time
1 2 3 4 5   2. Starts work on time
1 2 3 4 5   3. Finishes assignments
1 2 3 4 5   4. Participates in class discussions
1 2 3 4 5   5. Listens while others speak
1 2 3 4 5   6. Follows directions
1 2 3 4 5   7. Initiates self-improvement tasks
1 2 3 4 5   8. Begins work without delay
1 2 3 4 5   9. Can work independently
1 2 3 4 5   10. Works cooperatively with others
1 2 3 4 5   11. Puts away materials
1 2 3 4 5   12. Uses class materials appropriately
1 2 3 4 5   13. Other _____

The checklist might be completed by a student as a self report. The same checklist could also be given to the student's teachers or friends. Comparisons might be made. In some instances, the instruments might be a starting place to explore feelings and behaviors.

In addition, other sources of information can also be used to provide evidence about a person's development or behavior. Grades, school attendance, achievement, aptitude tests, and teacher record books are some traditional sources that might be used. Sociograms could be used to learn more about a student's relationships with others.

**Facilitator Skills and Concepts**

Assessment of facilitator skills and concepts is a natural expectation of both students and trainers. How much have the students learned in the training sessions? What gaps in their knowledge of the helping process still exist? How do they feel about their abilities and the abilities of other facilitators? Can they recognize the difference between helping and non-helping behaviors? Are the facilitators able to put their knowledge and skills into a working form so that they can engage in some projects?

These and other questions could be answered by administering some pencil-paper inventories and tests. Role-playing might be used to observe the use of skills and a checklist used to record competencies. In many cases, decisions about helping projects are based upon the results of measuring facilitator skills.

The *Facilitator Competency Test (FCT Parts I and II)*. The *FCT Part I* in Figure 7.4 can be administered at the conclusion of the beginning phase of training (Sessions 1-10). It consists of multiple choice items and open ended situations to which students respond in writing. The items and situations are meant to be illustrative. Others could be substituted or added.

### Figure 7.4
### Facilitataor Skills and Concepts Test
### (Part I — For Beginning Facilitators)

**Directions:** For each of the following, circle the best answer.

1. Which of the following is not one of the four helping characteristics?
   a. Caring            c. Understanding     e. Accepting
   b. Protecting        d. Being Trustworthy

2. Which of the following tells about what careful listeners should do?
   a. Look at the person who is talking.
   b. Pay attention to the person's words.
   c. Be aware of the person's feelings.
   d. Say something that show's listening.
   e. All of the above.

3. Lisa said, "I haven't any friends since I've come to this school." What is the word which best describes her feelings?
   a. Excited           c. Lonely            e. Annoyed
   b. Angry             d. Comfortable

4. John says, "My teacher always yells at me, but a lot of other kids talk without permission and she doesn't say a word to them. What word best describes his feelings?
   a. Picked-on         c. Scared            e. Lonely
   b. Happy             d. Proud

5. Vince says, "Since that big dog chased me, I won't walk home that way again. I could get hurt." Which word best describes his feelings?
   a. Strong            c. Pleased           e. Confused
   b. Mad               d. Scared

6. Ann says, "I don't mind all this rain, I get to stay indoors and work with my dad! Which word best describes her feelings?
   a. Confused          c. Bored             e. Discouraged
   b. Excited           d. Relaxed

7. Which of the following best describes people who have problems?
   a. Criminals         c. Principals        e. Everyone
   b. Presidents        d. Students who fight

Assessing and Evaluating Progress

8. Friendly helpers who understand others
    a. are able to focus on the feelings.
    b. were there to see what happened.
    c. had the same thing happen to them.
    d. saw a television program about it.
    e. read a book about people's problems.
9. A careful listener will look
    a. directly at the person who is talking.
    b. away from the person who is talking.
    c. at the person's hands most of the time.
    d. at the person, if the talk is interesting.
    e. at the person's feet most of the time.
10. When a person is talking, you should
    a. pay attention to the person's words.
    b. think about what you would have done.
    c. think if you have ever had a similar experience.
    d. decide what the best advice might be.
    e. not let them talk too long.
11. Feelings are best described as
    a. good and bad.
    b. pleasant and unpleasant.
    c. right and wrong.
    d. yours and mine.
    e. his and hers.
12. Which of the following is the least facilitative response?
    a. feeling-focused statement.
    b. clarifying and summarizing.
    c. open question.
    d. a "thank you for sharing" response.
    e. advice.
    e. telling someone what to do.
13. Which of the following is an open question?
    a. Did you say that?
    b. Are you going there?
    c. What could you say?
    d. Can you tell us?
    e. Do you want to go?

14. Which of the following is a feeling-focused response?
    a. You are a nice person.
    b. You are discouraged with the results.
    c. Which way are you going now?
    d. If I'm following you, it was an easy test.
    e. You need to talk with the counselor.

Facilitators who have completed all training sessions might be prepared to take the *FCT Part II* (Figure 7.5). Again, students respond to multiple choice items and open ended situations. These are related to concepts and skills associated with the intermediate and advanced training sessions.

### Figure 7.5

### Facilitator Skills and Concepts Test

### (Part II — For Intermediate and Advanced Facilitators)

**Directions:** For each of the following, circle the best answer.

1. One thing we know about problems is:
    a. few people have them.
    b. not everyone has them.
    c. rich people don't have them.
    d. everyone has them.
    e. only young people have them.
2. Feedback is
    a. telling other persons your opinion of them.
    b. critizing other persons actions.
    c. calling them a name.
    d. telling them they are right or wrong.
    e. telling them the feelings you get when they do something.
3. The difference between complimenting and confronting is
    a. one is right and the other is wrong.
    b. one centers on pleasant feelings and the other on unpleasant feelings.
    c. compliment only if the person is nice.
    d. confront only if you know the person well.
    e. there is no difference.

Assessing and Evaluating Progress

4. Your self-image is
   a. the name you use in school.
   b. what you think of yourself.
   c. how others would describe you.
   d. what your parents think of you.
   e. what you want to be someday.
5. Beliefs and attitudes:
   a. cannot be changed.
   b. influence the way you make decisions.
   c. are different for boys and girls.
   d. can never be known.
   e. are right or wrong.
6. Which of the following was *not* described as a student helping role:
   a. tutor
   b. special friend
   c. student assistant
   d. small group leader
   e. counselor
7. A facilitator is
   a. someone who helps people think about ideas and feelingss.
   b. a number in a math problem.
   c. a baseball player.
   d. a police officer.
   e. someone who has a lot of answers to problems.

Instructions for 8 - 12: List the five steps of the *problem-solving model*.

8. _____
9. _____
10. _____
11. _____
12. _____

Read the situations below and follow the directions for each.

13. Three girls are walking behind you. You don't know them very well. Suddenly, you trip, your books and papers tumble across the floor. The girls help you pick up the books

and papers. They are friendly. Give them some feedback. Underline step one, circle step two, and draw two lines under step three.

14. You are a tutor to John. He is learning to multiply. Today, for the first time, he has the correct answers to all of the flash cards you are showing him. You are proud of him. Give him some feedback.
15. Some friends keep trying to talk you into doing something that you don't want to do. Think of an example and give them some feedback.

**Evaulating Skills With Tape Recordings.** Tape recorders could be used by students in their projects or in role-playing or practice situations. You might:

1. Show the students how to use the recorders, including volume and tone controls, microphone position, pause button, and digital counter.
2. Demonstrate the use of the recorder in a role playing interview.
3. Encourage or assign each student to make a clear tape recording.
4. Tell the students to listen to their tapes and, using the counter, to make notes of where certain statements or dialog take place.
5. Ask them to write a reaction to their recorded notes, perhaps a statement about each of their responses in terms of kind, purpose or their feelings and ideas.
6. Encourage them to share their recordings and notes with each other, perhaps in pairs or triads.
7. Help them look for the positive aspects of their work and not to dwell on "mistakes" or "regrets."
8. Recommend that they periodically take 5 minute samples from their tape recordings and analyze their own progress. A tally card (Figure 7.6) might be helpful.

**Figure 7.6**
**Facilitator Skills Tally Card**

Tape _____

|  | First Part | Middle Part | Last Part |
|---|---|---|---|
| Questions |  |  |  |
|   Closed |  |  |  |
|   Open |  |  |  |
| Clarifying |  |  |  |
| Feeling-focused |  |  |  |
| Feedback |  |  |  |
| Problem-Solving |  |  |  |
|   Step One |  |  |  |
|   Step Two |  |  |  |
|   Step Three |  |  |  |
|   Step Four |  |  |  |
|   Step Five |  |  |  |
| Advice |  |  |  |

Ask students to provide you with a sample of their work in various projects. You could use a tally card to give them some feedback about their work and keep records of their progress and needs.

In one program students recorded several of their meetings with other students in helping projects. Grace, a sixth grader with advanced training, analyzed her own recordings with a second grade girl. Figure 7.7 contains her log entries for the last session.

## Figure 7.7

### Side One, Tape 3 — Grace and Melissa

I think I did okay, but I asked too many quesitons and in the beginning I was interrupting her. I know I put myself down a lot on this paper, but I still think I did pretty good.

| Counter Number | Comments |
|---|---|
| 6 | - |
| 9 | I got off the subject |
| 19 | Good |
| 25 | I don't know what I'm talking about |
| 49 | Should have told her ahead of time she was being taped—I thought I did |
| 62 | I heard wrong. Not getting anywhere. I thought she said people say she lies and she really said someone was hitting her in line. (But, she really does lie a lot.) |
| 71 | A feeling response. Good for me! |
| 88 | Telling her what to do. . . It's a habit. . . I'm her classroom patrol! |
| 111 | Good! Asking her how she feels |
| 115 | What? I've got to get my hearing tested. |
| 127 | Good! Asking her if she wants my ideas (But, I've been giving a few along the way already—should have waited) |
| 140 | Shouldn't have told her that (Didn't know you were going to hear!) |
| 169 | Good! I told her she didn't have to do it. |
| 193 | The end! |

Student facilitators are often more critical of themselves than are trainers. They want to do well and are eager to prove themselves. Having them analyze their own work is a learning exercise that teaches them self-discipline and to assume responsibility for their behavior. In addition, it encourages them to analyze their work when a supervisor is not present. This is an important goal, since it is impossible to assess or evaluate all student work.

You may also want to caution students about treating their recordings with care. Recordings should not be shared outside of the facilitator group unless permission is received from the student who is being taped. To do so would be unethical and risk the trust relationship.

**Direct Observation.** The same general procedures described above might be modified for direct observation. For example, you could observe a facilitator leading a small group discussion. Using the checklist, the leader's responses could be charted and later shared in supervision. Or, you might pair students in a co-leading experience, with one facilitator leading the group while the other records observations. Then, they could switch roles. Video tapes add an extra source of information and could also be used if available.

In one instance, a facilitator and a helpee sat in a circle for a conversation. Other facilitators watched the practice session from their position in an outside circle. This "fishbowl" technique is stressful to some, especially at first, but it also provides direct observation of skills.

Others who are in a position to observe the work of students can also help. For example, teachers who are supervising an area in which facilitators are working could take notes on behaviors and offer reactions. They could use the checklist, if they are familiar with the concepts and skills.

**Facilitator Effectiveness**

Fourth and fifth grade students were trained in a beginning facilitator program to be small group leaders in a second grade. The project was entitled "My Friends and Me" (See Chapter VI). After the four small group sessions in the classroom, the second graders were asked to express their thoughts anonymously on a survey instrument, the *Facilitator Effectiveness Test* (Figure 7.8). As the teacher read the questions, students in the class indicated their degree of agreement by marking one of five different faces that were based upon a Likert-type scale.

Likewise, other inventories might be developed which would enable helpees to express their ideas about facilitators. Helpees might be interviewed or asked to write a brief response to some open-ended questions: What did you like best? Least? What has resulted, if anything? How would you describe your facilitator? What would you say to others about the experience (or program)? What did you learn? Would you want to work with the person again? Why?

Facilitator effectiveness can also be assessed with the help of attendance records, grades, achievement scores, classroom behavior checklists, self-concept inventories, and so forth. For example, if a facilitator is involved in a tutoring project with a young boy or girl, then the number of assignments completed, handed in, or self-initiated could be used to report student progress. Similarly, helpees could keep a record of their own progress (See Figure 7.3).

## Figure 7.8

### Facilitator Effectiveness Test

**Directions:** Pass out the answer sheets and read the following to the second grade students after the circle sessions have been completed.

"You are the only one who knows how you think and feel about some things. I am going to read you some sentences asking about the group leaders and circle groups that you have been in. You will put an "X" on a face to show how much you agree or disagree with each sentence I read to you. There are no right answers, we are only interested in how you think or feel.

Now, look at the faces on the first page. Notice that the face on the far left has a big smile. If you strongly agree with the sentence that I read, you would put a big "X" on that face. The next face has a little smile. You would put your "X" on that face if you agree with the statement, but don't strongly agree. The middle face is not smiling or frowning—it is in-between. Put your "X" on this face if you feel unsure about the sentence. The next face has a little frown. Put your "X" on this face if you disagree with the statement. And, the last face has a big frown. Put your "X" on this face if you strongly disagree with the sentence."

**1st Example:** Let's try an example. Put an "X" on the face in the first row which shows how you feel about this sentence, "I like chocolate ice cream." (repeat)

(Pause) Who would like to share which face they put the "X" on?

**2nd Example:** Let's try another example. In the second row on this page, put your "X" on the face which shows how you feel about the following statement. "I like to get up in the morning." (repeat)

(Pause) Are there any questions?

Turn to the next page and we'll begin with number one. (Read each statement aloud and repeat over.)

The following are the twenty statements to which students respond on their answer sheets.

1. Being in my circle group was fun.
2. I learned how to be a better listener from my group.
3. I learned something about others in my group.
4. I'm glad I was in my group.
5. I think my group leader liked me.
6. I would like to have more groups in my class.
7. My group leader was a good listener.
8. I learned something about myself in my group.
9. My group leader was helpful.
10. I learned how to be a better friend in my group.
11. My group leader understood what I said.
12. Others in my group learned something about me.
13. I would like to talk with my group leader again, sometime.
14. I told others about my feelings.
15. My group leader liked what I said in the group.
16. I was listened to in my group.
17. Everyone had a chance to talk.
18. It was okay to tell my feelings.
19. I would like to be a group leader, someday.
20. People in our class are friendlier because of the groups.

Each student answer sheet consist of twenty two rows of faces. The first two rows are for students to respond to the examples. The other twenty rows correspond to the twenty statements read to the students.

The following is a sample row of faces:

## Program Evaluation

Finally, you will want to assess or evaluate the over-all impact of the program. All of the assessment instruments and devices mentioned above can be used to collect information for this kind of evaluation. Or, other instruments might be used. A case study, with names deleted or changed, might be one interesting way to approach accountability. Charts showing positive gains in a situation also impress those who are trying to learn more about your program. You might examine all of the evidence accumulated and develop a slide presentation around which the information could be presented. School board members, administrators, community organizations, parents, or newspaper reporters will be interested in your findings.

A video-taped demonstration project might also be used to illustrate some of the program's outcomes. For instance, a tape might show brief excerpts of students working in all four helping roles. It could conclude with testimonials for some students who worked with the facilitators. Teachers might also be interviewed and some of their remarks included.

You could have your own journal in which you make notes of student progress as you observe it during the program. These notes help in planning future projects and in making judgments about program effectiveness. Recording your feelings as well as observations make the journal more personal and useful.

Finally, you could also ask an outside observer to interview students and observe their work. Their evaluation might take the form of a research project, perhaps one in which the county or district personnel would be involved.

Systematically collecting information is one of the most neglected aspects of most programs. Make your plans early and follow through with them. Include a brief final report that can be distributed to administrators and interested persons in the community.

# Chapter VIII
# Trainers as Facilitators and Learners

Regardless of how many ideas might be suggested for a student facilitator program, the final outcome will be determined by the trainer or coordinator. It is the trainer who decides what facilitators will learn and the projects that will be undertaken as a group. It is the trainer or coordinator who must lead the way in working with the school faculty so that facilitators can take active roles in helping others.

Are you ready to be a trainer or coordinator? What attitudes and skills do you have at this point? What are your expectations? What's in it for you?

The *Trainer Rating Scale* (Figure 8.1) can help you determine whether or not you are ready to start a program. It will help you take a closer look at yourself.

### Figure 8.1
### Trainer Rating Scale

**Directions:** For each of the following items, rate yourself on how much you agree or disagree. Circle a "1" if you strongly disagree, a "2" if you disagree, a "3" if you are unsure, a "4" if you agree, or a "5" if you strongly agree. Be as candid with yourself as you can.

I am...

1 2 3 4 5   1. feeling burned-out.
1 2 3 4 5   2. understanding of student needs and interests.
1 2 3 4 5   3. full of extra energy.
1 2 3 4 5   4. don't like how others in school see me.
1 2 3 4 5   5. doubting if I could be a good trainer.
1 2 3 4 5   6. above average in counseling skills.
1 2 3 4 5   7. above average in group leader skills.
1 2 3 4 5   8. knowledgeable of communication theories.
1 2 3 4 5   9. well-liked by students.
1 2 3 4 5   10. respected by the school faculty.
1 2 3 4 5   11. discouraged with my job.
1 2 3 4 5   12. respected by the principal.
1 2 3 4 5   13. wondering if I can organize a program.
1 2 3 4 5   14. wondering about what my parents might say.
1 2 3 4 5   15. willing to give students more responsibilities in learning.
1 2 3 4 5   16. enthusiastic about the potential of a facilitator program.
1 2 3 4 5   17. committed to a facilitator program.

Now, let's take a closer look at your ratings. All of the items have significance, but some have more than others when you are starting or further developing a program.

Certainly, it helps to have an understanding of student needs and interests (No. 2) and to be liked by students (No. 9). That's a nice place from which to start. It also helps if you are already in favor with the faculty, principal and parents (No. 10, 12, and 14). However, student facilitator programs have a way of bringing you some positive recognition and additional respect. You are going to become more popular with students and others in the school.

You will develop close relationships with a few students and other students will want to work with you. Some will be envious if not included at first and ask when they can be in the program. It is likely that more students will want to be in the program after the first year and you will probably feel more pressure to give more students some training.

It is not uncommon for teachers and counselors to feel burned-out these days (No. 1). They sometimes wish they had more energy (No. 3) and might even be suspicious of those who seem to have extra energy when the day's work is done. Some are discouraged with their jobs (No. 11) and no longer look forward to their work. More than a few have become negative about education, schools, students and the future.

Recently, student facilitator programs have been described in some professional conventions as a way of combating the stress and frustration of teaching and counseling. For instance, one convention program was entitled: "Feeling Burned-Out? Then Change Gears and Try Peers." Another read: "Burned-out? Lacking Energy? Discover a New Resource—Student Facilitators." Presenters spoke from personal experience and described how their programs were energizing to themselves and their students. Others with similar experiences were quick to agree.

A student facilitator program can provide you experiences that are a high point of the day. It incorporates the best of educational theory and methods. There is generally more excitement and feelings of accomplishment because students are so responsive. You will like your job better than before.

You might be concerned about your own communication or counseling skills and concepts (No. 6, 7, and 8) and wonder if you can teach students something you find difficult to practice yourself. Or, you may have even reached a point of wondering whether or not your teaching or counseling abilities are slipping. That can happen at times, especially given the difficult tasks and limitations facing so many professionals in the schools.

Self-doubt can be an anchor in trying to get a program underway. Yet, trainers and coordinators report that they learn to be better counselors and teachers by teaching students. As you help students learn basic helping skills, you sharpen your own skills and abilities. You practice them with your students. You can try new ideas with them. You and your students can explore problem moments, consider alternatives and look for more ways to approach a situation. You too can benefit from the exploration process. Reviewing the concepts in this book and the basic skills associated with the program tends to make you more effective in your job.

If you are wondering whether or not you can be successful with student facilitators (No. 5) and put together an organized program (No. 13), then this book can be used as a reliable guide to help you through some first steps. The ideas and practices will help you be successful in achieving your goals. Other ideas will grow out of your experiences and you can add or substitute those later. Start with the basics and begin small, letting the program evolve. Take your time. Have patience with students and with yourself, as you move toward a comprehensive program.

No doubt all of the items on the rating scale can play an important role in your decision to develop a program. All of them can influence the progress that you make. All of them will improve as a result of your work with a facilitator program. However, experience has suggested that the last three items (15, 16, and 17) should receive the most attention at this point. These items focus upon your commitment, enthusiasm and willingness to risk with students.

Your willingness to give students more responsibilities in the learning process (No. 15) is one item that should be examined carefully. This is the heart of the idea, the soul of the program. After training, you will have to trust your students and your judgment.

Close supervision, especially at first, can ease this unsureness. But, if you smother students with it then they will feel too constrained and lose enthusiasm. You must first believe that children can help children, sometimes more effectively than adults can help children. Giving students responsibilities, especially when they are prepared for them, enhances self-confidence, feelings of competence, and the ability to assume more responsibility.

Enthusiasm can take you a long way (No. 16). It is often contagious and others enjoy the excitement and positiveness that come with it. When people are enthusiastic, they frequently communicate self-confidence and inspire others. There is also a fun and light-hearted aspect about enthusiasm that is appealing. Those who take an idea too seriously can sometimes create added stress that only a few can tolerate for long periods of time. Helping others is serious business, but it should be with interest and enthusiasm rather than with a solem face of determination.

Likewise, commitment to start or further develop a program (No. 17) is a critical variable that deserves special attention. Half-hearted efforts are usually perceived that way and they rarely encourage others to identify with them, applaud them, or talk about them. They are usually followed with resistance, skepticism, and a lack of involvement.

Yet, when commitment is present things begin to happen. There is less avoidance of tasks that must be done. There is more attention to details. Changes take place and are sustained. For example, commitment separates world class athletes from those that might have been. It makes winners out of some who would have otherwise been also-rans. It gives meaning to the extra effort that is sometimes needed to achieve and it helps one take pride in the little gains that are made toward a goal.

With commitment you can find ways to gain support, create projects for students, work through schedule conflicts, and provide the assistance that students need in learning to help others. Commitment also has an element of patience and persistance. It creates focused energy that is necessary to start a program on its way and sustain its momentum. For that reason, it was cited as the first step in building a program (Chapter III).

Take a closer look at items 15, 16 and 17 again. If the sum of your scores for those three items is less than 12 points at this time, then you may want to re-read this book or talk with others about your ideas before starting. Or, you may want to pass this book on to someone else whom you can encourage and support as a trainer. If your score averaged four or more on these items, then you are ready to begin as trainer, facilitator and learner.

## Being a Successful Trainer

Myrick and Erney (1979) described the person responsible for a student facilitator program as trainer, facilitator and learner. They outlined some characteristics of a successful trainer and concluded:

> Being the person responsible for the training and supervision of student facilitators is a challenging, rewarding, and personal learning experience. It is challenging because of the interpersonal skills that must be taught, the questions that demand answers and the decisions that must be made. It is rewarding because it enhances the lives of hundreds of young people who experience some very special attention and caring as a result of the program. Finally, it is a personal learning experience for the trainers because the trainers must re-evaluate their professional skills, develop new ones and, at the same time, clarify their own value systems (p. 197).

As trainer or coordinator of the program, it is your responsibility to structure most of the learning experiences for the facilitators and those with whom they work. You select training activities and design experiences for them. You will make the final decisions about helping projects. Ultimately, the responsibility of the program and the work of the facilitators rests with you. In addition you will aslo be in the role of facilitator. Like the students you train, you will be facilitating others toward more personal growth and development. You will facilitate leadership.

Leadership is not something that can be defined and taught easily. It's almost impossible to tell people how to be a leader. Rather, leadership is a collection of skills that is molded into a personality style that appeals to others. As a facilitator you lead through modeling the helping skills.

Although you introduce learning activities, interpret them on occasion, and give firm directions at times, as a facilitator you encourage students to learn by feeling, talking and doing. Rather than provide quick answers, you can facilitate their thinking about a situation, some alternatives and consequences, and encourage them to be responsible decision-makers. As a facilitator you can be most effective as trainer and friend.

Finally, you will also be in the role of learner. You will learn a lot more about yourself through the program. Be open to the experience. Take some risks to get the program implemented. Admit to yourself when you are uncertain or anxious about a situation. You may want to share those feelings with someone else or the students themselves.

You need not cast yourself as a perfect model, or as someone who never makes mistakes. This role doesn't hold well in the long run, no matter who tries it. In the process, it can also be intimidating to others. All of us make mistakes and learn from them.

As you and your students try new ideas and experiment together, discuss your frustrations and excitement. While working with the students, take your turn to facilitate, to share ideas, and to perform tasks. They will respect you more for it. Keep your sense of humor and enjoy the learning experience because it will make some positive differences in your life.

## The Case of James

James was a sixth grade boy who had difficulties in school. He seemed to be in trouble most of the time with his peers and teachers. Although some students thought that James was "funny" at times and found his antics entertaining, most of them avoided or ignored him on the playground and after school. Some were afraid that James would pick on them or would get them into trouble.

The school counselor in James' school had experimented with a peer facilitator group the previous year and decided to expand the idea. He wanted to develop a student facilitator program, one in which more students would be involved with more helping projects. In this program students would become known as junior counselors (Bowman & Myrick, 1980). He had no idea that it would lead to a fateful encounter with James.

> I can remember the first time I learned about James. Mrs. Colson was pulling her hair out over him. All she could say was, "What are we going to do with that boy? What in the world can we do?" She would shake her head in bewilderment.
>
> When I looked in James's cummulative folder, it was easy to see that he had been of concern to all of his previous teachers. Each had written something about his disruptive influence in the class and noted that he was working below his potential. His aptitude scores on standardized tests suggested that he was above average, especially in verbal skills. Yet, his school grades were barely passing.
>
> When I talked with James individually he seemed a likeable boy with a charming smile. But, it was obvious that he was unhappy in school. He mentioned on several occasions that his teachers didn't like him. He often told me things like, "They are always picking on me— I know I do things sometimes that bother them but, other kids do things too...And I'm the one that always gets blamed for everything. It's not fair.!"
>
> James' teachers reported that he worked just enough in class to get by and used a lot of his time daydreaming, drawing cartoons or bothering other students. One teacher exclaim, "The kid's a nightmare for me! But then on some days I really wonder what's going on with him—he can be a nice kid when he wants to be."

In January, I made a tour of the upper grade classes and told them that I was planning to expand the facilitator group. It would be a "Junior Counselor" program where those selected could work with and help others. The students had heard about last year's group and were eager to hear more about my plans. I knew a lot of kids would apply. But, I had no idea that such an experience would appeal to James. Here is what he said on the form I asked students to complete:

### Why I Want to Be a Junior Counselor

*I want to be a Junior Counselor because. . . I like little kids and I want to help them. I know what it's like to have problems, cause I have had some. This is the only thing I ever wanted real bad to do in school. Please, please, please, let me be one of these helpers! I'll be good and work harder than anybody!!!!*

*James W.*<br>*Room 221*

Working with three groups was going to be difficult enough. There was no need to ask for headaches, especially with a boy like James who was unpredictable, except when it came to his being disruptive or distractable. He was hardly my idea of the best student for some of the projects I had in mind.

His enthusiastic comments, however, caught me by surprise. Frankly, my first thought was that his interest was a ploy to get out of class. Maybe it was just an excuse to goof-off in another part of the school. Yet, there was something about his expressed interest that also caused me to wonder what he had on his mind.

A few days later it was James' turn to be interviewed for the program, a process that helped me select students and also heighten student enthusiasm. During the interview, James' behavior was subdued. He seemed so sincere and promised to "do the best he'd ever done."

Although I had my doubts, it also struck me that perhaps he could benefit from the experience. Training would be treatment. He could be a target student receiving some extra attention through the program. It would be different from the counseling approaches that had been attempted before by me and others before me. It just might work. Besides, he could always be asked to leave if things didn't work out.

James was thrilled to be selected. He rushed home and told his parents who became confused. His mother called me and asked if James was in trouble again. After I explained the purpose of the program, she was delighted that he would get a chance to participate. But, the tone of her voice suggested that she had some doubts about James too.

During the first training session, James sat next to Jerome, a boy who sometimes befriended him and who was also a special case. I wondered if they should be separated, but both contributed to the discussion without disruption and I forgot about the idea. Later, I wondered how long the "honeymoon stage" would last.

The group members brought lists of feeling words that they had compiled for the fourth training session. A minimum of 35 words was requested as an assignment. James' list totaled 74 and included little drawings of faces beside each word to show how the feeling was expressed. He also told how he had watched *Roots* on television that week and kept note of the feeling words. He made a log and also wrote words that he heard while watching *Mork and Mindy*. James was certainly off to a good start, or so it seemed.

The next day, James asked if he could talk privately with me. He was worried about something. When we met I learned that his teacher, Mr. Carson, had told him that he "hadn't changed one bit" and James was not going to be allowed to attend the training sessions anymore if he "messed up" one more time.

I met with Mr. Carlson after school and talked with him about James. When I showed him that list of feeling words, he shook his head in disbelief. "Well, at least someone is getting something out of that kid." He decided to work more closely with me and to encourage James when he could. He also agreed to let James talk with him about some matters and to be tape recorded as part of a project. While the tape didn't show ideal communication between them, it definitely helped clear the air and pave the way for some important changes.

Two weeks later, Mr. Carlson wrote me a note saying that James was "really shaping up." He had turned in all but one assignment that week. Further, he was working on his assignments in class—and without bothering others! I suggested that he send a similar positive report home with James to his parents. Mr. Carlson agreed and said, "It's probably the first positive note the kid has ever taken home to his parents."

James continued to improve both in class and in the training sessions. He bubbled with enthusiam and was eager to take part in some helping projects. He used a recorder to tape a conversation that he had on the playground with a third grade boy. It showed how hard he was trying to use helping responses. Later, he practiced his skills with his little sister. He became a model in our group and gained the respect of other members. The other students didn't say much about it but they were obviously warming up to a "new" James.

After some advanced training, including practice with a problem-solving model, James was given an opportunity to talk with a classroom teacher who had volunteered for a helping project. Mrs. Arnold was a fourth grade teacher who didn't know James, except what she had heard from other teachers. She agreed to meet James after school and tell him about an actual problem that she was having with some of the students in her class. The counselor encouraged her to express real concerns and not to role play.

The next day James checked out a tape recorder and visited Mrs. Arnold's room. He introduced himself. "Mrs. Arnold, I heard that you would like to talk with me about a problem that you are having in your class." She smiled and said, "Well, yes...I guess I do."

Mrs. Arnold later confided how she enjoyed talking with James and was surprised how helpful the brief session had been. She laughingly said, "I learned something. . . and I originally thought I was just going to help James."

As the year passed, James was involved in several other projects. For example, he became a "special friend" to two second grade boys who frequently started fights with others on the playground. James became a kind of hero to them. He also became a tutor to a third grade boy who was behind in math. Working with the boy also helped James to concentrate more on his own math.

Two weeks before the end of the school year, the Junior Counselor group of facilitators met for a final session. It was to be a party and celebration for all their hard work. Each student brought something— a decoration or refreshment. As part of the preparation, different student groups spent a week writing lyrics for songs that represented their feelings and experiences as facilitators. I brought in a guitar and played some different styles of music for each song—country western, rock and roll, and soft ballad—depending upon each group's wish. While it wasn't "solid gold" the lyrics gave an impression of how much they all had enjoyed the program. It was a very emotional time for me and I still remember that last meeting as if it were yesterday.

James? He continued to improve in all areas of school. His final report card showed one and two letter grade improvements in his subjects. Mr. Carlson became one of James' best supporters and enjoyed some friendly teasing with him as the year moved along.

It's been almost two years since I've seen James. Recently, I received his tenth letter about his experiences in junior high school. Three of his letters described how he had become friends with a boy who could not walk and who used a wheel chair to get around in school. James wrote, "I did a lot of listening. . . and I sure learned a lot too." James also reported that his grades have been consistently Bs on his recent report cards. His interest in school is obviously continuing to climb.

James will always hold a special place in my heart. He learned a lot about helping others that year .

## What Other Trainers Have Said

— "It's really fun. And, I get such a kick out of watching the kids work with each other. I probably shouldn't be amazed, but I am."

— "I never dreamed these kids would learn so fast. I can't imagine why we haven't been teaching them more about communication skills and facilitating others before now."

— "I've been trying peer helper programs for a long time. Some years I've been more diligent at it than others. But, I agree with a systematic approach—it can make the difference."

— "I've learned to be a better counselor through teaching the skills to students. It's just another case of really learning something when you have to teach it to someone else."

— "I had some very special feelings for my kids. We shared some neat things together and I'm going to miss them when they go on the the middle school."

— "There is still a lot of room for improvement in my program. I know that. But, the rewards have already been worth the trouble I had in getting a few teachers to cooperate."

— "It's probably the best part of my school counseling program."

— "One day I was feeling down. Things didn't go right and when I arrived at school it must have showed. Linda said, 'Hey, you sure look down today.' Her comment caught me by surprise. I sat down and talked with her for a little bit and even more surprising—the little talk helped. I was proud of her and glad I gave her the chance to facilitate me that day."

## What Others Have Said

**Parent:** "That's all Andy talks about these days— his friendly helper group. He comes home and tries it out on us. It's made a difference in his attitude about school."

**From a Group of Teachers:** "Well, one conclusion that I think we all reached was that students can be more helpful to each other. They can also be of help to us. We probably should have started this a long time ago."

**Teacher:** "Frankly, I worried—especially at first— about the students leaving my class. But, I've since learned that it isn't a waste of time. It's a good experience for all the kids."

**Princil:** "I'd say it's one of the best programs that we have in the school." (He also listed it on a memo to the supertendent as one of the ten best things that were happening in his middle school.)

**Parent:** "One of the most interesting things that happened since Diane became a helper, or whatever you call it—is that we have had some good talks together. She seems more grown-up and takes more interest in the family."

**Parent:** "I like listening to Andrea talk about the class (facilitator group) and I've learned somethings from what she's said. I support it and think other kids could learn something from it too."

**Teacher:** "It's been a helpful experience for my students, although not all of them have improved in their school work... but some have. The kids look forward to working with the big kids and that's something I've used to motivate them to get their work done on time."

**Teacher:** "Joanna is such a shy little girl. She hardly talks and then only in a whisper. I tried getting her to talk more, but she doesn't have much self-confidence. Andrew (a student facilitator) has been working with her as a friend and tutor. I think it's making a difference. At least she smiles more these days."

**Teacher:** "I really don't know who it helps the most or even if some kids get anything out of it... but I can tell you one thing... it's been great for Ulla, our little girl from Sweden... Just really great!"

Trainers as Facilitators and Learners

## And Now...

Children helping children is one of the most significant educational concepts that has received special attention within the last few years. Through student facilitator programs many young people can be trained or prepared to help others. They can learn to be leaders and role models for each other. They can be taught to be effective assistants, tutors, group leaders and friends.

As students learn to facilitate the personal and academic growth of themselves and others, educational programs can become more effective and learning will be enhanced. You can play a valuable role in assisting children to help children. And now... is the time to start!

# Appendix

## Supplemental Activities — Chapter I
## Learning About Resistance

**Purpose:**

To explore the nature of resistance in the helping process.

**Materials:**

Small bowl, cup of cornstarch, water, spoon or stirring stick, and moist towel.

**Procedures:**

1. Pour a cup of cornstarch in the bowl and slowly add water, stirring slowly until it forms a very thick paste.

2. Ask one student at a time to forcefully poke or tap a finger on the surface of the mixture as though in a hurry to force the finger to the bottom of the bowl. (The dough will resist swift movements and react like a solid.)

3. This time ask the students to slowly ease their fingers into the dough until they touch the bottom. (The cornstarch will be less resistant and will react like a liquid.)

**Discussion:**

1. What happened when you tried to force your fingers in the cornstarch? How might this be similar to helping people?

2. What happened when you slowly eased your fingers into the cornstarch? How is this similar to helping people?

3. What is resistance?

4. If you noticed a third-grade boy or girl who was sad and alone, what are some beginning statements that you could make that might cause resistance? What are some beginning statements that might meet with less resistance?

## Feeling Word Search (II)

**Purpose:**

To identify feeling words and build feeling word vocabulary.

**Materials:**

Ready-made copies of the block of letters or a master chart which students may copy themselves, pencils, and a dictionary.

**Procedures:**

1. Students may work on this activity individually or in groups.

2. You might say:

   "Each letter is part of one or more words which describe feelings. Words may be spelled forward, backward, up, down, or diagonally. Find each one and circle it. There are 29 feeling words in this chart of letters. Here is a hint: every letter except '**X**' is part of at least one feeling word.

3. An optional procedure might be to give students the list of 29 words and have them locate each one on the chart.

| L | D | U | O | R | P | C | A | L | M |
|---|---|---|---|---|---|---|---|---|---|
| S | O | R | R | Y | X | X | B | X | A |
| T | W | N | E | A | T | D | I | R | D |
| I | N | T | E | R | E | S | T | E | D |
| R | N | N | N | L | X | A | T | J | I |
| E | O | A | T | X | Y | D | E | E | S |
| D | D | T | H | E | A | X | R | C | C |
| D | E | S | U | F | N | O | C | T | O |
| S | K | I | S | R | G | S | X | D | U |
| H | C | D | E | E | R | X | E | D | R |
| Y | I | X | D | E | Y | O | N | N | A |
| X | P | B | O | R | E | D | X | X | G |
| H | U | R | T | U | N | S | U | R | E |
| R | E | P | U | S | C | A | R | E | D |

256      Children Helping Children

| | |
|---|---|
| 1. Lonely | 16. Picked on |
| 2. Down | 17. Unsure |
| 3. Distant | 18. Rejected |
| 4. Proud | 19. Sorry |
| 5. Angry | 20. Bored |
| 6. Tense | 21. Calm |
| 7. Interested | 22. Mad |
| 8. Settled | 23. Shy |
| 9. Enthused | 24. Tired |
| 10. Confused | 25. Free |
| 11. Bitter | 26. Sad |
| 12. Annoyed | 27. Neat |
| 13. Discouraged | 28. Hurt |
| 14. Scared | 29. Super |
| 15. Sure | |

**Discussion:**

1. How are feeling words different from other kinds of words?
2. Which of the words describe pleasant feelings? Unpleasant feelings?
3. How many of the feeling words in the chart have you experienced?
4. Which words are unfamilar or new to you? What do the words mean?

## Supplemental Activities — Chapter II
## The Gossip Game

**Purpose:**

To learn the value of listening and how repeating information can distort an original story or statement.

**Materials:**

A short paragraph that tells a story about someone. For example:

> "Mr. Josephson told the boy who worked in his shop that a lady left her brown purse on the counter top near the coke that spilled. He was suppose to call her and return it."

**Procedures:**

1. Set up an "experiment" with the group. Begin by having everyone, except one person, leave the room.

2. Read the story to the student who remains in the room — other students can learn later exactly what was said. Read the story only once.

3. Then, bring in a second student from outside. The first student, to whom you told the story, now tells it to the second one.

4. This person tells it to a third student who is called in, and so on until all have heard the story. The last person tells the group the story and this is compared to the story as it was read by you.

**Discussion:**

1. How much distortion took place from the beginning to the end?

2. How is this related to other kinds of communication in school that takes place?'

3. What can be done to reduce distortions?

4. What part does listening play in conversation? What part does memory play?

5. How is "gossip" like this experiment?

## Ten Questions

**Purpose:**

To provide a structured listening experience for students in which they practice asking questions and listening for information.

**Materials:**

None.

**Procedures:**

1. Place students in pairs, preferably with someone they know least in the group. Have them find a private place in the room.
2. Each person asks two questions of the other person. Then, two more questions are asked in turn. Finally, one last question is asked (thus, each person asks five questions of a partner). Questions are of one's own choosing, but the other person has the right "to pass" on any question.
3. After all questions have been asked and answered, each student takes one minute to summarize what has been learned about the other person.

**Discussion:**

1. What was the most interesting question your partner asked you?
2. Do questions help you to know someone better? What if that is all a person does in talking with you?
3. What kind of questions were most helpful in getting to know the person better?
4. If you could play *Ten Questions* with a famous person, who would it be? What would be five questions?

## Supplemental Activities — Chapter III
## Pass the Pencil

**Purpose:**

To practice the three helping responses and to develop listening skills.

**Materials:**

Pencil or some object that can be passed.

**Procedures:**

1. Students sit in a circle. One member, called the "pencil-holder" is the only one who may speak.
2. The first pencil-holder makes a few statements about a recent experience. Other students in the group use careful listening.
3. The pencil is passed then to any one of the other group members who makes a response. This response might first be an open question, or some other response requested by the leader.
4. The group discusses the response to the pencil holder, perhaps brainstorming other responses that might have been made.
5. The student who made the response becomes the new pencil holder. Another round begins as this student makes a few statements about a recent experience. The pencil is passed again, and another response is received.
6. This procedure continues until everyone in the group has had at least one opportunity to respond. Or, it might continue until a competency is achieved for a certain skill.
7. This is not a go-around. Rather, the pencil-holder surprises someone by giving that person the pencil. The activity can be used to progressively build the helping skills, perhaps moving from open questions to feeling-focused responses. Or, it might be spontaneous where any response may be given and the group is asked to identify it.

**Discussion:**
1. Which of the helping responses needs more practice?
2. How did you feel when you were given the pencil without notice. How did passing the pencil effect the group's listening?
3. How could this activity be used in a helping project?

### H.O.T. Triads (Helper, Observer and Talker)

**Purpose:**

To provide additional practice with the helping responses.

**Materials:** Paper or checklist for observer, pencil.

**Procedures:**
1. Divide the students into triads.
2. Ask each triad to assign one student to be the "talker" who will talk briefly about a situation. A second student in the triad becomes the "helper" who uses the three helping responses to help the talker explore feelings and thoughts. The third student is the "observer" who sits to the side and records the helper's responses and who later tells what was observed.
3. Allow about three minutes for talkers to share an experience. Then another two or three minutes might be used for the observers to tell their observations.
4. Ask the students to exchange roles and repeat the exercise, until each has been in all three roles.
5. Sometimes a topic can be given by the trainer to which all talkers share their thoughts (e.g. Something I would like to change; Something about myself that I like; A decision I'm trying to make.)

**Discussion:**
1. Which of the helping responses do you still need to practice?
2. What other kinds of responses entered into the process?
3. Was it easier to be the talker, the helper or the observer?
4. What was "hot" about the triads—what did you like or dislike about the experience?

## Supplemental Activities — Chapter IV
### Dear Abby

**Purpose:**

To help identify problems that young people have and to recognize how feelings and behaviors are related.

**Materials:**

Small cards or slips of paper, pencils

**Procedures:**

1. Introduce the activity by bringing a newspaper that contains a "Dear Abby" column. Ask the students, "What can you tell me about Dear Abby?" Emphasize how the column is used to tell a problem and get advice, or to "get something off your mind," and to learn that others have problems too.

2. Then say, "Today we are going to begin our own form of 'Dear Abby.' Start by writing down a question or problem that you have, a problem someone you know is having, or one that you think would be interesting to discuss. By the way, I'll probably include a few that I've learned from talking with others your age." Students do not sign their names on the cards or slips of paper.

3. Collect the cards and read one problem aloud for the group to discuss. Here are some that have been included:

    Others tease me because I'm skinny.

    I have a bad temper that gets me into trouble.

    I have to take care of my little sister all the time.

    My mom won't let me play football. She treats me like a baby.

    The person who sits next to me keeps cheating.

4. Focus the discussion on: a) how it would feel to have a problem like the one read aloud and b) what do people do when they feel that way (thus, linking feelings and behavior). Avoid giving advice. Leave that to Abby. The goal is to increase respect and understanding rather than brainstorm solutions.

## Discussion:

1. How are feelings related to behavior? If a person feels "sad" in a situation, what are some things that person would probably do that would tell us about the sadness?

2. If you are angry, do you act angry? What else can be done to express anger?

3. How can knowing how you feel make a difference in the way a problem is solved?

## Alternatives and Consequences

### Purpose:

To practice thinking of alternatives and consequences to problems.

### Materials:

Paper, pencils/pens.

### Procedures:

1. Have students find their own private places in the room. Tell them to divide their papers in half with a vertical line.

2. Read a situation like one of the following.

    A. "You are an explorer alone in a dark jungle. Suddenly, a herd of wild elephants comes charging toward you and you begin to run. Soon, you come to the edge of a deep gorge. The cliff in front of you is too steep to climb down and you have no rope. The elephants are close behind and still charging. What can you do?

    B. You are the first person your age to win a million dollars in a contest. What can you do with your money?

    C. You rub an old lamp. A genie appears and tells you that you can have all the wishes you can think of in three minutes. But, each one must help to make the world a better place. What will you wish?

3. Give them about three minutes to write as many alternatives as they can, listing them on the left sides of their papers.

4. Next, give them 2-5 minutes to write, in the right columns of their papers, a possible consequence for each idea if it were chosen and acted upon.

5. Re-group the students and let them share some of their alternatives and consequences. Ask the group to identify similarities.

6. If time allows, ask each student to rank order the top three and decide which ones to use for the plan.

**Discussion:**

1. To which step of the problem-solving model is this activity related? In what ways?

2. How can taking the time to focus on alternatives and consequences help you to make more responsible decisions?

3. Think of a concern that you have. How helpful would it be to think more about the alternatives and consequences?

## Supplemental Activities — Chapter V
## Feedback Go Around

**Purpose:**

To practice giving and receiving positive feedback and to help students learn more about themselves and others.

**Materials:**

None.

**Procedures:**

1. Have the students sit in a circle. If your group is larger than seven, put them into two groups. Or, you could assign students to small triads. The activity seems to work best with about five or six in a group.

2. Review the three parts of the direct feedback model. These parts or steps might be posted on a chart or chalk board for easy reference, if students are still unsure of them.

3. One student volunteers to begin and speaks in turn to each of the others in the group. After giving all members of the group some feedback, another person volunteers and goes around the circle, giving everyone some positive feedback. The person receiving the feedback simply says "Thank you" or nods showing that the student was heard. However, there is no discussion until everyone has finished.

    It might help if you tell the volunteers to: a) call the persons by name, b) look at them, and c) talk directly to them not about them.

4. After the last person has practiced giving feedback, have the group discuss the experience. You should take a turn too, both giving and receiving feedback. If some students want to focus on the same behavior or situation, let them do so even though somone else gave attention to it first. The feedback will still be personal and different.

5. This could also be an open experience, without the restriction of a positive focus. In that case, the cautions about confrontation might be reviewed.

**Discussion:**
1. How did you feel when giving feedback to people in the group?
2. Was it easier to give or receive feedback? Was it easier with some people than with others?
3. Did you follow the feedback model? What order of the steps did you use?

### Positive Superlatives

**Purpose:** To provide positive feedback.

**Materials:** Name tags, pens or markers.

**Procedures:**
1. Give the group approximately 5-8 minutes to arrive at some positive superlatives or names. Students must reach some general consensus that each member in the group is "The Most (or Best) _", which is positive. For example, one member might be seen as the "most friendly" and another "the most willing to help others" or "the best athlete." The student for whom the group is trying to decide a superlative does not take part in the discussion but listens.
2. As soon as all the positive superlatives have been determined for the group members, a description tag is pinned or taped on each one of them.
3. Next, the group members tell each person about some of the things that led to the name or tag. Students tell why they believe a tag is appropriate based on their own experience.
4. After everyone has learned more about the name given them, the group discusses their feelings about the experience.

**Discussion:**
1. Can people have more than one superlative? Can superlatives change?
2. What is a superlative that you would like to have, besides the one you were given? What would you need to do to earn that kind of tag?
3. How are these kind of tags different from the feedback model?

## Supplemental Activities — Chapter VI
## Circles, Squares or Triangles?

**Purpose:**

To facilitate thinking about prejudice, stereotyping, and feelings of superiority, and to demonstrate the value of cooperation.

**Materials:**

Pre-cut triangles (10), circles (10), and squares (10), using a different color for each of the three shapes. Paper, pencil/pen.

**Procedures:**

1. Divide the students into three groups.
2. Give one group the set of circles, the second group the squares and the other group the triangles. Allow about 4 to 5 minutes for each group to list reasons why their shape is better than other shapes. Make sure that the students hold and think about the shape for their group.
3. Then, each group uses their one shape to form a picture on the floor or desk.
4. Bring all the students together and listen to each group's list and look at the group's picture. Lead a discussion, focusing on feelings and behaviors.
5. Next, assign students to different groups, so that all three shapes are represented in each group.
6. Ask the new groups to use a combination of their pieces to make a picture (e.g. spaceships, sunsets, futuristic cars, flowers). These will be more colorful and interesting than the previous pictures because more shapes and colors are represented.
7. Have each group tell about their picture.

**Discussion:**

1. How were the arguments for superiority of the shapes the same and different for each of the groups?
2. How are these arguments applied or used with people?
3. What was the difference when groups worked with all shapes together? What feelings and behaviors were the same or different?

## The Ideal Student

**Purpose:**

To explore some behaviors that make an "ideal student" and to assess one's self in terms of those behaviors.

**Materials:**

A large piece of paper, (perhaps newsprint), where a person's body could be traced to provide a form of a student. Magic markers, slips of paper and masking tape.

**Procedures:**

1. After tracing a student, post the paper with masking tape. Title the picture, *The Ideal Student* and ask the group to think of things that an ideal student would do. Focus the discussion on behaviors.

2. Using the marker, write the ideas directly on the picture or on slips of papers that could be taped or pasted on.

3. After the group has listed or taped the behaviors on the picture, ask the group how each one is like and not like the ideal student.

4. Have each student select two things that they do which are the most like the ideal student and two that need improving upon.

**Discussion:**

1. Is an ideal student always perfect? What does an ideal student do more than most other students?

2. What is the value of working toward being an ideal student?

3. What can you do in the near future to become more of an ideal student?

4. Would your teachers agree or disagree with your selections?

## Supplemental Activities — Chapter VII
## Unfinished Sentences

**Purpose:**

To explore thoughts and feelings about student facilitator roles.

**Materials:**

Each student will need six small pieces of paper to write on—perhaps a notebook paper torn into six parts, pen/pencils.

**Procedures:**

1. Ask each student to find a place in the room to write answers privately. Make sure each has six pieces of paper.
2. Inform them not to write their names on the papers. Responses will be read to the group anonomously.
3. Read an unfinished sentence—one listed below or one of your own. Ask students to complete the statement on one of their pieces of paper. If they can't think of anything, they may write "pass," but encourage them to try answering each one.
4. Before reading the next unfinished sentence, collect the responses to form one pile.
5. Continue this procedure until you have six piles, one for each statement.
6. Reassemble the group and lead a discussion of each response. The group might come up with suggestions, ideas, or encouraging comments for each sentence.
7. The following six unfinished statements might be used.

    A. I'm still worried about...

    B. What if...

    C. I might need more practice with...

    D. I still don't quite understand...

    E. I hope that I don't...

    F. I hope that others will...

## The Helping Roles

**Purpose:**

To give students an opportunity to think more about the helping roles before choosing a project.

**Materials:**

Paper, pencils/pens.

**Procedures:**

1. Review briefly the four helping roles (i.e. student assistants, tutors, special friends, and small group leaders).
2. Form smaller groups and have each group brainstorm projects, or ways in which these roles might be used around school or home.
3. After about 5-6 minutes, ask the groups to share their ideas, looking for similarities and differences. You may want to add some ideas to the lists. Each role should have at least three ideas.
4. Next, ask each student to select one favorite idea for each of the four roles.
5. Then, have the students individually rank order their four choices.
6. Lead a discussion in which the students share their choices.

**Discussion:**

1. Which of the roles seem to have the most ideas for projects?
2. Which one role seems to be the favorite of the group?
3. What is a project in which these roles might be performed?
4. What are some individual projects (or group projects) that can be performed spontaneously? That need to be organized and planned for?
5. What is a project in which more than one role may be combined?

# List of Recommended Resources
## For Trainer and Coordinator

### Films

Myrick, R.D., & Sorenson, D.L. *Developmental Counseling in the Elementary School* (30-minute 16mm color film). Minneapolis, MN: Educational Media Corporation, 1976.

Myrick, R.D., & Sorenson, D.L. *The Middle School Years: Guidance for Transition* (30-minute l6mm color film). Minneapolis, MN: Educational Media Corporation, 1978.

Myrick, R.D., & Sorenson, D.L. *Peer Facilitators: Youth Helping Youth* (27-minute l6mm color film). Minneapolis, MN: Educational Media Corporation, 1976.

Myrick, R.D., & Sorenson, D.L. *Leading Group Discussions* (27-minute l6mm color film). Minneapolis, MN: Educational Media Corporation, 1978.

### Books and Modules

Canfield, J.C., & Wells, H.C. *100 Ways to Enhance Selfconcept in the Classroom: A Handbook for Teachers and Parents*. Englewood Cliffs, NJ: Prentice-Hall, 1976.

Dinkmeyer, D. *DUSO I & II (Developing Understanding of Self and Others)*. Circle Pines, MN: American Guidance Service, 1970 & 1973.

Gray, H.D., & Tindall, J. *Peer Counseling*. Muncie, IN: Accelerated Development, Inc., 1978.

Morrison, K., & Thompson, M. *Feeling Good About Me*. Minneapolis, MN: Educational Media Corporation, 1980.

Myrick, R.D., & Erney, T. *Caring and Sharing: Becoming a Peer Facilitator*. Minneapolis, MN: Educational Media Corporation, 1978.

Myrick, R.D., & Erney, T. *Youth Helping Youth: A Handbook for Training Peer Facilitators*. Minneapolis, MN: Educational Media Corporation, 1979.

Palomares, U. *Human Development Program (Magic Circle).* La Mesa, CA: Human Development Training Institute, 1970.

Pfeiffer, W., & Jones, J. *A Handbook of Structured Experiences for Human Relations Trainers, 7 Volumes.* La Jolla, CA: University Press, 1973-1979.

Samuels, D., & Samuels, M. *The Complete Handbook of Peer Counseling.* Miami, FL: Fiesta Publishing Corp., 1975.

Wittmer, J., & Myrick R.D. *Facilitative Teaching: Theory and Practice (Second Edition).* Minneapolis, MN: Educational Media Corporation, 1980.

# Bibliography

Allen, V.L. *Children as Teachers: Theory and Research on Tutoring.* New York: Academic Press, 1976.

Allen, V.L., & Feldman, R.S. Learning through tutoring: Low-achieving children as tutors. *Journal of Experimental Education*, 1974, *42*, 1-5.

A.S.C.A. Newsletter. Peer counseling. 4/1/79, *16* (2 and 3), 12-13.

Anderson, R. Peer facilitation: History and issues. *Elementary School Guidance and Counseling*, 1976, *11* (1), 16-25.

Baker, J. Big friend: A tutorial program. *Educational Leadership,* 1973, *30*, 733-735.

Berenson, G.B., & Carkhuff, R.R. *Source of Gain in Counseling and Psychotherapy: Readings and Commentary.* New York: Holt, Rinehart and Winston, 1967.

Bowman, R.P. The peer facilitator movement: Its impact on our schools. *Florida Personnel and Guidance Association Guidelines*, 1980, *25* (2), 2.

Bowman, R.P., & Myrick R.D. I'm a junior counselor, having lots of fun. *School Counselor*, 1980, *28* (1), 31-38.

Briskin, A.S., & Anderson, E.M. Students as contingency managers. *Elementary School Guidance & Counseling*, 1973, *7* (4), 262-268.

Brown, W.F. Student-to-student counseling for academic adjustment. *Personnel and Guidance Journal*, 1965, *43*, 811-817.

Caditz, R. Using student tutors in high school mathematics: Weak students profit from volunteer assistance. *Chicago School Journal*, 1963, *44*, 322-325.

Canfield, J.C., & Wells, H.C. *100 Ways to Enhance Self-concept in the Classroom — A Handbook for Teachers and Parents.* Englewood Cliffs, NJ: PrenticeHall, 1976.

Carkhuff, R.R. *The Art of Problem-Solving.* Amherst, MA: Human Resource Development Press, 1973.

Carkhuff, R.R., & Berenson, G.B. *Beyond Counseling and Therapy.* New York: Holt, Rinehart and Winston, 1967.

Carkhuff, R.R., & Truax, C.B. Training in counseling and psychotherapy: An evaluation of an integrated didactic and experiential approach. *Journal of Counseling Psychology*, 1965, *29*, 333-336.

Carkhuff, R.R., & Truax, C.B. Lay mental health counseling: The effects of lay group counseling. *Journal of Counseling Psychology*, 1965, *29*, 426-431.

Carkhuff, R.R., & Truax, C.B. Toward explaining success and failure in interpersonal experiences. *Personnel and Guidance Journal*, 1966, *46*, 723-728.

Cicirelli, V.G. The effect of sibling relationship on concept learning of young children taught by child-teachers. *Child Development*, 1972, *43*, 282-287.

Cloward, R. Studies in tuturing. *Journal of Exceptional Education*, 1967, *36*, 14-25.

Devin-Sheehan, L., Feldman, R.S., & Allen, V.L. Theory & research on cross-age and peer interaction: A review of the literature. *Review of Educational Research*, 1976, *46* (3), 355-385.

Dinkmeyer, D. *DUSO I & II (Developing Understanding of Self and Others)*. Circle Pines, MN: American Guidance Service, 1970 & 1973.

Duncan, J.A. Ethical considerations in peer group work. *Elementary School Guidance and Counseling*, 1976, *11* (1), 59-6l.

Duncan, J.A., & Gumaer, J. *Developmental Groups for Children*. Springfield, IL: Charles C. Thomas, 1980.

Edwards, S.S. Student helpers: A multilevel facilitation program. *Elementary School Guidance and Counseling*, 1976, *11* (1), 52-58.

Ehlert, R. Kid counselors. *School Counselor*, 1975, *22* (4), 260-262.

*Elementary School Guidance and Counseling. Special Issue: Peer Facilitators, 1976, 11* (1), 1-80.

Erickson, M.R., & Cromack, T. Evaluating a tutoring program. *Journal of Experimental Education*, 1972, *41*, 27-31.

Ettkin, L., & Snyder, L. A model for peer group counseling based on role-playing. *School Counselor*, 1972, *19* (3), 215-218.

Feshbach, S., & Devor, G. Teaching styles in 4-year olds. *Child Development*, 1969, *40*, 183-190.

Frager, S., & Stein, C. Learning by teaching. *Reading Teacher*, 1970, 403-405.

Frank, M., Ferinand, B., & Bailey, W. Peer group counseling: A challenge to grow. *School Counselor*, 1975, *22* (4), 267-272.

Fredicine, A.J., & Kramer, C.R. SIA: Students in action. *School Counselor*, 1971, *19*, 133-135.

Freed, A.M. *T.A. for Kids.* Sacramento, CA: Jalmar Press, Inc., 1971.

Gartner, A., Kohler, M.C., & Riessman, F. *Children Teach Children: Learning by Teaching.* New York: Harper and Row, 1971.

Gibbs, J., & Allen, A. *Tribes.* Oakland, CA: Center Source Publications, 1978.

Gordon, T. *P.E.T. Parent Effectiveness Training.* New York: Peter H. Wyden, 1970.

Gray, H.D., & Tindall, J. Communication training study: A model for training junior high school peer counselors. *School Counselor*, 1974, *22* (2), 107-112.

Gray, H.D., & Tindall, J. *Peer Counseling.* Muncie, IN: Accelerated Development, Inc., 1978.

Gumaer, J. Peer facilitated groups. *Elementary School Guidance and Counseling*, 1973, *8* (1), 4-11.

Gumaer, J. *Peer facilitator training and group leadership experience with low performing elementary school students.* Unpublished doctoral dissertation, University of Florida, Gainesville, 1975.

Gumaer, J. Affective education through the friendship class. *School Counselor*, 1976, *23* (4), 257-263.

Gumaer, J. Guest editorial. *Elementary School Guidance and Counseling*, 1976, *11* (1), 4.

Gumaer, J. Training peer facilitators. *Elementary School Guidance and Counseling*, 1976, *11* (1), 26-36.

Hall, J., & Zener, A.E. *Youth Effectiveness Training.* Solana Beach, CA: Effectiveness Training, Inc., 1977.

Hamburg, B.A., & Varenhorst, B.B. Peer counseling in the secondary schools: A community health project for youth. *American Journal of Orthopsychiatry*, 1972, *42*, 566-581.

Hansen, J.C., Niland, T.M., & Zani, L.P. Model reinforcement in group counseling with elementary school children. *Personnel and Guidance Journal*, 1969, *47* (8), 741-744.

Hatch, E.J., & Guerney, B. Jr. A pupil relationship enhancement program. *Personnel and Guidance Journal*, 1975, *54* (2), 102-105.

Hoffman, L.R. Peers as group counseling models. *Elementary School Guidance and Counseling*, 1976, *11* (1), 37-44.

Houtz, J.C., & Feldhusen, J.F. The modification of fourth graders' problem solving abilities. *Journal of Psychology,* 1976, *93*, 229-237.

Jackson, G.G. In the field: Black youth as peer counselors. *Personnel and Guidance Journal*, 1972, *51* (4), 280-285.

Jacobs, E., Masson, R., & Vass, M. Peer helpers: An easy way to get started. *Elementary School Guidance and Counseling*, 1976, *11* (1), 68-71.

Kaplan, S.N., Kaplan, J.B., Madsen, S.K., & Taylor, B.K. *Change for Children.* Pacific Palisades, CA: Goodyear Publishing Company, Inc., 1973.

Keat, D.B. II. Training as multimodel treatment for peers. *Elementary School Guidance and Counseling*, 1976, *11* (1), 6-13.

Kelly, F.D. *The Differential Effects of Giving Versus Receiving Help in a Cross-Age Helping Program.* Unpublished doctoral dissertation, University of Florida, Gainesville, 1970.

Kern, R., & Kirby, J. Utilizing peer helper influence in group counseling. *Elementary School Guidance and Counseling*, 1971, *6* (2), 70-75.

Kum, W., & Gal, E. (Reported in "Programs in Practice"). *Elementary School Guidance and Counseling*, 1976, *11* (1), 74.

Lakin, D.S. Cross-age tutoring with Mexican American pupils. *Dissertation Abstracts International*, 1972, *32* (7-A), 3561.

Leibowitz, A., & Rhodes, D.J. Adolescent peer counseling. *School Counselor*, 1974, *21*, 280-283.

Lippitt, P., & Lippitt, R. Peer culture as a learning environment. *Childhood Education*, 1970, *47*, 135-138.

Mastroianni, M., & Dinkmeyer, D. Developing an interest in others through peer facilitation. *Elementary School Guidance and Counseling*, 1980, *14* (3), 214-221.

McCallon, E. *School Attitude Test.* Austin, TX: Learning Concepts, 1973.

McCann, B.G. Peer counseling: An approach to psychological education. *Elementary School Guidance and Counseling*, 1975, *9* (3), 180-187.

McCurdy, B., Civevich, M.T., & Walker, B.A. Human relations training with seventh grade boys identified as behavior problems. *School Counselor*, 1977, *24* (4), 248-252.

Melaragno, R.J. *Tutoring With Students: A Handbook for Establishing Tutorial Programs in the Schools.* Englewood Cliffs, NJ: Educational Technology Publications, 1976.

Mollad, R.W. Pupil-tutoring as part of reading instruction in the elementary grades. *Dissertation Abstracts International*, 1970, *31* (4-B), 2260.

Moore, W.G. *The Tutorial System and Its Future.* New York: Pergamon Press, 1968.

Morgan, J.J. Problem solving potential in elementary school children. *Child Study Journal*, 1976, *6* (1), 39-47.

Morrison, K., & Thompson, M. *Feeling Good About Me.* Minneapolis, MN: Educational Media Corporation, 1980.

Mosley, E.M. The case for guidance in elementary schools. *Elementary School Guidance and Counseling,* 1972, *6* (3), 151-152.

Myrick, R.D. Editorial: Peer facilitators: Youth helping youth. *Elementary School Guidance and Counseling*, 1976 *11* (1), 2-3.

Myrick, R.D., & Erney, T. *Caring and Sharing: Becoming a Peer Facilitator.* Minneapolis, MN: Educational Media Corporation, 1978.

Myrick, R.D., & Erney, T. *Youth Helping Youth: A Handbook for Training Peer Facilitators.* Minneapolis, MN: Educational Media Corporation, 1979.

Myrick, R.D., & Sorenson, D.L. *Peer Facilitators: Youth Helping Youth* (27-minute 16mm color film). Minneapolis, MN: Educational Media Corporation, 1976.

Myrick, R.D., & Sorenson, D.L. *Developmental Counseling in the Elementary School* (30-minute 16mm color film). Minneapolis, MN: Educational Media Corporation, 1976.

Myrick, R.D., & Sorenson, D.L. *The Middle School Years: Guidance for Transition* (30-minute l6mm color film). Corporation, 1978.

Myrick, R.D., & Sorenson, D.L. *Leading Group Discussions* (27-minutes l6mm color film). Minneapolis, MN: Educatioinal Educational Media Corporation, 1978.

Niedermeyer, F., & Ellis, P. Remedial reading instruction by trained pupil tutors. *Elementary School Journal*, 1971, (7), 400-405.

Norris, R., & Wantland, P. Brothers and sisters assist readers. *School and Community*, 1972, *58* (6), 8, 46.

Palomares, U. *Human Development Program (Magic Circle).* La Mesa, CA: Human Development Training Institute, 1970.

Pfeiffer, W., & Jones, J. *A Handbook of Structured Experiences for Human Relations Trainers, 7 Volumes.* La Jolla, CA: University Press, 1973-1979.

Rashbaum-Selig, M., & Lally, A. *Assertive Training for Young People.* Unpublished paper, 1975.

Rashbaum-Selig, M. Student patrols help a disruptive child. *Elementary School Guidance and Counseling*, 1976, *11* (1), 46-51.

Richards, S.L. *Developmental play with peer counselors.* Unpublished manuscript presented at 1979 Florida PGA Convention, Daytona, FL.

Rockwell, L.K., & Dustin, R. Building a model for training peer counselors. *School Counselor*, 1979, *26* (5), 311-316.

Rogers, C.R. The necessary and sufficient conditions of therapeutic personality change. *Journal of Consulting Psychology*, 1957, *21*, 95-103.

Rogers, C.R. The essence of psychotherapy: A client-centered view. *Annals of Psychotherapy*, 1959, *1*, 51-57.

Rogers, C.R. *On Becoming a Person.* Boston: Houghton Mifflin, 1961.

Rogers, C.R. The interpersonal relationship: The core of guidance. *Harvard Education Review*, 1962, *32*, 416-429.

Rogers, C.R. *A Way of Being.* Boston, MA: Houghton Mifflin Co., 1980.

Samuels, D., & Samuels, M. *The Complete Handbook of Peer Counseling.* Miami, FL: Fiesta Publishing Corp., 1975.

Simpson, L.A., & Pate, R.H., & Burks, H.M. New approach: Group counseling with trained subprofessionals. *Journal of College Placement*, 1973, *33*, 41-43.

Sprinthall, N.A., & Erickson, V.L. Learning psychology by doing psychology: Guidance through the curriculum. *Personnel and Guidance Journal*, 1974, *52*, 396-405.

Stone, G.L., & Noce, A. Cognitive training for young children: Expanding the counselor's role. *Personnel and Guidance Journal*, 1980 *58* (6), 416-420.

Thoresen, C.E., & Hamilton, J.A. Peer social modeling in promoting career behaviors. *Vocational Guidance Quarterly*, 1972, *20* (3), 210-216.

Toffler, A. *Future Shock.* New York: Random House, 1970.

Truax, C.B., & Carkhuff, R.R. The experimental manipulation of therapeutic conditions. *Journal of Consulting Psychology,* 1965, *29*, 119-124.

U. S. Department of Health and Human Services. *Status of Children, Youth, and Families* (DHHS Pub No—OHDS 80-30274), 1979.

Vassos, S.T. The utilization of peer influence. *School Counselor*, 1971, *18* (3), 209-214.

Vogelsong, E.L. Relationship enhancement training for children. *Elementary School Guidance and Counseling*, 1978, *12* (4), 272-279.

Vriend, T.J. High performing inner-city adolescents assist low-performing peers in counseling groups. *Personnel and Guidance Journal*, 1969, *47* (9), 897-903.

Wagner, P. Analysis of a retarded-tutoring-retarded program for institutionalized residents. *Dissertation Abstracts International*, 1973, *34* (5-A), 2426.

Weise, R. Diary of a peer facilitator program. *Elementary School Guidance and Counseling*, 1976, *11* (1), 62-66.

Winters, W.A., & Arent, R. The use of high school students to enrich an elementary guidance and counseling program. *Elementary School Guidance and Counseling*, 1969, *3*, 198-205.

Wittmer, J., & Myrick, R.D. *Facilitative Teaching: Theory and Practice, Second Edition.* Minneapolis, MN: Educational Media Corporation, 1980.

Wrenn, R.L., & Mencke, R. In the field. *Personnel and Guidance Journal*, 1972, *50* (8), 687-689.

Zunker, V.G., & Brown, W.F. Comparative effectiveness of student and professional counselors. *Personnel and Guidance Journal*, 1966, *44*, 738-743.